To Bill

With congratulations and sincere good wishes on attaining L.G.R. may you. enjoy many years in Office

Steve

A TREASURY OF
MASONIC THOUGHT

Freemasonry, a beautiful system of morality, veiled in allegory and illustrated by symbols.

AUTHOR UNKNOWN

A Treasury of
Masonic Thought

EDITED BY

CARL GLICK

Foreword by Charles W. Froessel

Introduction by William Sherwood

LONDON
ROBERT HALE LIMITED

Copyright © 1959, 1953 by Carl Glick
First published in Great Britain 1961
Reprinted 1972
Reprinted 1974
Reprinted 1976
Reprinted 1979
ISBN 0 7091 3408 8

Robert Hale Limited
Clerkenwell House
Clerkenwell Green
London EC1R 0HT

To the Memory of
My Father and Grandfather,
Master Masons and Builders

PRINTED AND BOUND IN GREAT BRITAIN BY
REDWOOD BURN LIMITED, TROWBRIDGE AND ESHER

Acknowledgements

Grateful acknowledgement is made to the following publishers, agents, authors, and copyright owners for permission to reprint in this volume poems and prose from the copyrighted works indicated below. The listing is alphabetical by authors.

THOMAS BAILEY ALDRICH, "Enamoured Architect of Airy Rhyme;" Houghton Mifflin Company. ULYSSES F. AXTELL, "Light, More Light;" *The New York Masonic Outlook*, April, 1930. JOHN KENDRICK BANGS, "The Kingdom of Man," and "A Philosopher;" Francis H. Bangs for the estate of John Kendrick Bangs. JOHN EDMUND BARSS, "A Mason's Greeting" from *Masonic Poems*, a volume of *The Little Masonic Library*; permission of Southern Publishers, Inc., Kingsport, Tennessee. WALTER H. BONN, "To a Friend" and "Toil" from *Some More Masonic Poems*, compiled by Charles Clyde Hunt; permission of Mrs. C. C. Hunt. JOSEPHINE B. BOWMAN, "The Voice of America" from *Masonic Poems*, a volume of *The Little Masonic Library*; permission of Southern Publishers, Inc., Kingsport, Tennessee. JULIEN BRYAN, "This I Believe" from the radio programme and newspaper syndicate conducted by Edward R. Murrow; copyright, 1952, by Help, Inc.; permission of Ward Wheelock for Help, Inc.

ANDERSON M. BATEN, "The Home," an excerpt from *The Philosophy of Life* by Anderson M. Baten; permission of V. I. Schwab. ROBERT J. BURDETTE, "Get Away From the Crowd;" permission of Mrs. Robert J. Burdette. GAIL BROOK BURKET, "Biography," "Doubt Not Thy Father's Care," "Compelled to Valour by Our Heritage," and "Prayer;" permission of author. JOHN BURROUGHS, "Waiting;" permission of Houghton Mifflin Company. FRANKLYN CABLE, "Grant Thy Light" from *The New York Masonic Outlook*, December, 1939; permission of publishers. CARL H. CLAUDY, "Armed," "Music," "Mine," "Source," and "Sonnet;" permission of author; lines beginning "Masonic charity is strong, kindly, beautiful," copyright February, 1925, by the Masonic Service Association of the United States; lines beginning "Prudence in Masonry means wisdom," "Temperance as a virtue applying to," and "Fortitude is not only physical courage," copyright August, 1950, by the Masonic Service Association of the United States; reprinted by permission. JOHN CLIFFORD, "The Anvil" from *Some More Masonic Poems*, Iowa Masonic Library, 1944, compiled by Charles Clyde Hunt; permission of Mrs. C. C. Hunt. A. CLUTTON-BROCK, from *The Ultimate Belief*, copyright, 1916, 1944; permission of E. P. Dutton and Co., Inc. D. W. CLEMENTS, "The White Leather Apron" from *Some More Masonic Poems*, Iowa Masonic Library, 1944, compiled by Charles Clyde Hunt; permission of Mrs. C. C. Hunt. JOHN B. CRAFT, "Just Being Happy" from *The New Age Magazine*, August, 1937; permission of publishers and author. FRANK CRANE, from *The Looking Glass*; copyright, 1917, by John Lane Co., 1945 by Dodd, Mead and Company, Inc.; permission of Dodd, Mead and Company, Inc. ERNEST CROSBY, "Life and Death" from *Swords and Ploughshares*, copyright, 1902, 1930; permission of Funk and Wagnalls Company.

HENRY NEHEMIAH DODGE, "He Is a Man—My Brother" from *The Masonic World*, Detroit, Michigan; permission of publishers. WILL ALLEN DROMGOOLE, "The Bridge Builder" from *Rare Old Chums*; permission of L. C. Page and Company. ABRAHAM FELT, "Give Us Thy Light" and "We Take Those Things We Gave Away," composed by Right Worshipful Abraham Felt, Past Master National Lodge No. 209, F. & A. M., New York; Past Master and Founder of Humanitas Lodge No. 1123, F. & A. M., New York; from *The Masonic Family* Magazine, January-February, 1952; permission of author. GEORGE H. FREE, "My Ashlar," "Builders Are We," "Just Friends," "What of Your Masonry?," "What Makes You a Mason?," and "The Work Divine;" permission of Mrs. George H. Free.

B. G. GALLAGHER, from *Color and Conscience*, copyright, 1946, Harper and Brothers; permission of publishers. J. GIERLOW, "The Habitation of the Grand Architect" from *Masonic Poems*, a volume of *The Little Masonic Library*; permission of Southern Publishers, Inc., Kingsport, Tennessee. JOHANN WOLFGANG VON GOETHE, prose selections from *Goethe Wisdom and Experience*, translated and edited by Hermann J. Weigand; permission of Pantheon Books. SIR WILFRED GRENFELL, from *The Adventure of Life*, copyright, 1942; permission of Houghton Mifflin Company. EDGAR A. GUEST, "Home," "How Do You Tackle Your Work?," "Myself," and "See It Through" from *The Collected Verse of Edgar A. Guest*, copyright, 1934, by The Reilly and Lee Company, Chicago; and "Lord, Make a Regular Man of Me" from *The Light of Faith*, by Edgar A. Guest, copyright, 1926, by The Reilly and Lee Company, Chicago; permission of author and publishers; "Only A Building," copyright by Edgar A. Guest, permission of author. DAVID GUYTON, "Fraternity" from *Some More Masonic Poems*, compiled by Charles Clyde Hunt, Iowa Masonic Library, 1944; permission of Mrs. C. C. Hunt.

PIERRE HARROWER, "Evening Prayer;" permission of author. H. L. HAYWOOD, prose selections from *The Newly-Made Mason*, *More About Masonry*, and *Revised Encyclopedia of Freemasonry*, The Masonic History Company; permission of author and publisher; "We Are Two Brothers" and "God's Freemasonry," permission of author; "Immortality" from *Grand Lodge Bulletin*, Grand Lodge of Iowa, A.F. and A.M., January, 1952; permission of author and publishers. WILLIAM ERNEST HENLEY, "Invictus;" permission of Macmillan London and St. Martin's Press. MONTFORT C. HOLLEY, "The Building Code" from *The New York Masonic Outlook*, November, 1952; permission of author and publishers. WILLIAM H. HUDNUT, "Quit You Like Men;" permission of author. CHARLES CLYDE HUNT, "Our Temple" and "King Solomon's Temple;" permission of Mrs. C. C. Hunt.

EDGAR A. JONAS, "God and Home and Country," permission of Edgar A. Jonas and Illinois Grand Lodge Proceedings for 1941. JOHN HENRY JOWETT, from *The Friend on the Road*, copyright 1922, 1950, Harper and Brothers; permission of the publishers. WALTER H. JUDD, excerpts from a talk delivered in New York in 1950 and published in *The New York Masonic Outlook*, October, 1952; permission of author and publishers.

CHARLES RANN KENNEDY, from *The Servant in the House;* permission of

Harper and Brothers. STEPHEN G. KETCHAM, "Just This Minute;" permission of author. RUDYARD KIPLING, "Banquet Night" from *Debits and Credits*, copyright, 1926, by Rudyard Kipling; reprinted by permission of Mrs. George Bambridge and Macmillan and Company Ltd. and "The Mother Lodge" from *The Seven Seas*, reprinted by permission of Mrs. George Bambridge and Methuen and Company Ltd. BLANCHE BANE KUDER, "Blue Bowl" from *April Weather*, copyright, 1922, 1950; permission of K. M. Brewer. W. A. KUNCE, "Good Deeds" from *The New Age Magazine*, October, 1933; permission of publishers.

JOHN GILLESPIE MAGEE, JR., "High Flight" from *New York Herald Tribune*, February 8, 1942; permission of publishers. DOUGLAS MALLOCH, "Always a Mason," "Be the Best of Whatever You Are," "Building," "Echoes," "Father's Lodge," "The Little Lodge of Long Ago," "The Road of Masonry," "Today;" permission of Mrs. Douglas Malloch. EDWIN MARKHAM, "A Creed," "Brotherhood," "Duty," "Earth is Enough," "Man-Making," "Opportunity," "Outwitted," "Rules for the Road," "The Day and the Work," "The New Trinity," "Two at a Fireside;" permission of Virgil Markham. WALTER MALONE, "Opportunity" from *Selected Poems*, copyright, 1905, 1933; permission of Alba R. Malone. CARL W. MASON, "A Mason" from *The Virginia Masonic Journal*, 1916; permission of publishers. NEAL A. McAULAY, "The Apron Symbolism" and "The Five Points of Symbolism" from *Some More Masonic Poems*, Iowa Masonic Library, 1944, compiled by Charles Clyde Hunt; permission of Mrs. C. C. Hunt. LEWIS A. McCONNELL, "Peace, Unity and Plenty" from *Some More Masonic Poems*, Iowa Masonic Library, 1944, compiled by Charles Clyde Hunt; permission of Mrs. C. C. Hunt. RUSSELL J. McLAUCHLIN, "The Laying of the Cornerstone," "The Gauge," "The Gavel," and "The Level" from *Songs of the Craft*, copyright, 1927, by *Masonic News*; permission of publishers. H. MacPHERSON, "A Brother As Pilot" from *The Kraftsman*, November, 1933; permission of publishers. ANGELA MORGAN, "Work—A Song of Triumph" and "When Nature Wants a Man" from *Gold on Your Pillow;* permission of author. A. CRESSY MORRISON, from *Man Does Not Stand Alone*, copyright, 1944; permission of Fleming H. Revell Company. ERNEST S. MOORE, "The Absent One" from *Some More Masonic Poems*, Iowa Masonic Library, 1944, compiled by Charles Clyde Hunt; permission of Mrs. C. C. Hunt.

WILBUR D. NESBIT, "A Day of Thanksgiving," "The Good Word," "Be On Guard," "I Sat in a Lodge with You," "Your Flag and My Flag," and "Good Fellowship;" permission of Mrs. Wilbur D. Nesbit. JOSEPH FORT NEWTON, from *The Builders*, copyright, 1914, 1930, by Joseph Fort Newton; permission of Macoy Publishing and Masonic Supply Company.

MAX OTTO, from *Things and Ideals*, copyright, 1924; permission of Henry Holt and Company, Inc. HUGH ROBERT ORR, "They Softly Walk;" permission of author. EVART EMERSON OVERTON, "Light" from *The New York Masonic Outlook*, April, 1939; permission of publishers.

NORMAN VINCENT PEALE, from *A Guide to Confident Living*, copyright, 1948, by Prentice-Hall, Inc., New York, N.Y.; permission of publishers. WILLIAM

The journey of a thousand miles begins with one step.

LAO-TSE

FOREWORD

THE material progress of man in the past century is without parallel in all human history. Yet during this period we have had our own Civil and Spanish-American Wars, participated in two World Wars and the Korean War, witnessed a variety of lesser wars, and suffered a catastrophic world-wide economic depression. While presently passing through a so-called cold war, which flings its icy threats into the news of every day, we have found ourselves on the brink of war on several occasions, of which Suez, Lebanon, Jordan, Matsu and Quemoy, and now Berlin, are illustrations. Today, two conflicting ideologies are seeking to gain the mastery of men's minds.

Meanwhile, we are told by the United Nations that two-thirds of the world's population is illiterate, and close to two billion people are either near the starvation line or seriously undernourished. And forty million babies are added to the world's population each year!

Is it not a time to pause—and think? Our material progress has not solved life's problems nor the problems of nations. In many ways it has increased them. We would not return to the old methods of transportation and communication nor to the many discomforts of the years gone by. Yet, while our mechanical age has revolutionized man's way of living, human nature remains much the same. Thus the rules of conduct laid down by the great and earnest leaders and thinkers of the past ought not unthinkingly be discarded for much of the easygoing, loose self-persuasions of today.

It is well then, is it not, to take another look at the writings and thoughts expressed by our forebears and contemporaries, great and humble, for the rules of human behaviour undergo little change.

Carl Glick in his *Treasury of Masonic Thought* has helped us do just that. It is an interesting compilation not only of thought expressed in prose and poetry by Masons, but by non-Masons as well who have consciously or unconsciously expressed the Masonic concept of universal brotherhood under the Fatherhood of God. In my travels over the face of the earth, I have found countless Masons and non-Masons of every faith and creed who endeavour to live by this concept—in Europe, South America, Africa, Asia, the Near and Middle East, Australia and New Zealand, as well as in the United States of America and Canada. In a lodge in Rangoon, Burma, where I visited in 1956, there were nine Bibles representing nine different faiths on a single altar—truly a manifestation of brotherhood.

One finds unrest almost everywhere, but behind it one discerns the dreams and hopes and ambitions of people, particularly in the remoter areas of the world, to enjoy a greater measure of the freedom, liberty and progress of the so-called Western democracies. In these critical days, when earnest leaders are endeavouring to bring people more closely together as members of a great human family and to resolve the many conflicts among them, there must be more than material progress; otherwise we shall fail in the challenge facing our generation.

To find within the covers of a single volume so much of the wisdom of the past and present—stimulating and thought-provoking gems of literature that compel us to think of the spiritual side of man's existence, rather than merely his material progress—is not only deeply satisfying and inspiring but helps us to think unselfishly about our relationship with other members of the human family. It is a welcome and wholesome addition to the books of any home or library.

Charles W. Froessel

Augus 28, 1959

INTRODUCTION

THROUGHOUT the ages the world's greatest writers have expressed universal fundamental truths. These truths Freemasonry has embodied in its teachings, philosophy, thoughts, and ideals. Freemasonry makes no claim to have originated these everlasting truths, but it is the aim of every sincere and true Mason to practise them in his everyday living.

So here is a collection of poetry and prose, the wisdom of the ages and the echoes of that wisdom by living writers, an expression of Masonic thought. While the selections included are of special significance to Masons, this book can also be read and enjoyed by their families and friends. The principal tenets of Freemasonry are so fundamentally universal that they belong to all men in all times and all nations. In building this collection it is obvious that the editor had two basic points in mind.

First he selected very definite expressions of Masonic thought from the writings of some of the world's greatest men of letters who were themselves Masons. Among these writers will be found Robert Burns, James Boswell, Lord Chesterfield, William Cowper, Goethe, Rudyard Kipling, Edwin Markham, Sir Walter Scott, Friedrich von Schiller, Benjamin Franklin, Tolstoy, Alexander Pope—to mention only a few. While some of these writers did not always write about Masonry as such, there can be found in their writings truths which the Mason will recognize as flowing from the fountainhead of Masonic philosophy and teaching. In addition have been included selections from lesser known Masonic writers, whose devotion to Masonry springs from their hearts. Some may not even be known to the world, yet these writers are of great stature in Masonic circles. So in this collection, as in a Masonic Lodge, the humble sit side by side with the great.

This collection also contains selections from writers who were not themselves Masons. These have been included because the editor, satisfied that the thoughts expressed in these selections are based on eternal truth, has found in them echoes of the dynamic principles and tenets of Freemasonry.

So it is entirely within the character of Freemasonry that the world of letters bears the imprint of its philosophy and teaching. Its humanitarian aims, its formal principles and ritual, are all etched across the centuries on wings of poetry and prose. That poetry predominates is not unexpected, for there is little written within the tens of thousands of volumes of Masonic literature that is not set down in the measured meters of poetry. And often even that which appears as prose bears the planned structure of a poem.

This is only right, since the Mason's art has been the Builder's craft. Although the origin of Freemasonry extends to the mists of antiquity, the most ancient records indicate that as early as the thirteenth century Freemasons were builders. Builders usually of cathedrals, they were free men who moved unmolested across Europe during the Middle Ages in their work of creating buildings of stone dedicated to the Great Spiritual Builder in the Heavens.

The Freemasons of today dedicate their intangible building tools as a living testimony to the Glory of their Spiritual Buildings above. Rare is the written work worthy of the name of literature—be it poetry or prose—that does not dedicate itself to the improvement of the heart, mind and soul. It is for that reason that the compiler of this collection has placed emphasis on those selections which have most appealed to him, as demonstrating the higher virtues, and man's relation to humanity.

The emblem—the visible insignia of the Mason—is itself composed of instruments of the builder's art. The Square, the Compass, all in geometric design, indicate the great objective in the building and re-building of man's character and man's work with man. No longer does the Freemason work with stone and the mason's tools. Today their endeavours are charged with improvement and self-building to the end that actions, words and deeds approach the perfection asked for by the Spiritual Builder.

And so in this book is found poetry and prose of inspiration not only for Masons but all who wish to reach for higher attainments and the true spiritual growth inherent in all mankind.

All human beings turn their faces to that time when they shall be judged by their works and deeds. Mankind travels by many roads, often different roads, but in the end they all lead to the appointment with the Heavenly Auditor. Freemasonry with its building skill provides a chart of the Traveller's course—a way that if closely followed tends to gain favour in the final audit.

William Sherwood, P.M.

St. John's Lodge, No. 1
A.Y.M.—F. & A.M.,
New York, N.Y.

CONTENTS

Authors in this Collection Known to be Masons

Ethan Allen
Ulysses F. Axtell

David Barker
John Edmund Barss
Walter H. Bonn
James Boswell
Edward Bulwer-Lytton
Robert Burns
William Jennings Bryan

Franklin Cable
Lord Chesterfield
William R. Clapp
Carl H. Claudy
Samuel L. Clemens
D. W. Clements
John Clifford
William Cowper
John B. Craft
Frank Crane
Cummings

Stephen Decatur
Henry Nehemiah Dodge

Herbert N. Farrar
Abraham Felt
Charles F. Forshaw
Benjamin Franklin
George H. Free

J. Gierlow
Johann Wolfgang von Goethe
J. Q. Goss
Lawrence N. Greenleaf
Edgar A. Guest
David Guyton

Alexander Hamilton
Nathan Hale
Pierre Harrower

H. L. Haywood
Fay Hempstead
Patrick Henry
Montford C. Holley
Charles Clyde Hunt

John J. Ingalls

J. M. Jenkins
Edgar A. Jonas
Walter H. Judd

Charles Rann Kennedy
Stephen G. Ketcham
Rudyard Kipling
W. A. Kunce

Franklyn W. Lee
Gotthold Ephraim Lessing

Charles Mackay
Douglas Malloch
Edwin Markham
Neal A. McAulay
Lewis A. McConnell
Russell J. McLauchlin
H. McPherson
John Marshall
Carl W. Mason
Giuseppe Mazzini
Ernest R. Moore
Robert Morris
Wolfgang Amadeus Mozart

Wilbur D. Nesbit
Joseph Fort Newton

Evart Emerson Overton

Norman Vincent Peale
Albert Pike
Alexander Pope

W. W. Riley
Will Rogers
Theodore Roosevelt

Michael N. Salmore
Friedrich von Schiller
J. Hubert Scott
Owen Scott
Sir Walter Scott
W. R. Shields
George B. Staff

W. J. Thompson

Count Leo Tolstoy
Arthur S. Tompkins
Salem Town

John W. Vrooman
Voltaire

Lew Wallace
George Washington
Thomas Smith Webb
A. W. Witt

Giles Fonda Yates

Let There Be Light

LET YOUR LIGHT SHINE

I would not give much for your Masonry unless it can be seen. Lamps do not talk, but they shine. A lighthouse sounds no drum, it beats no gong, and yet far over the water its friendly spark is seen by the mariner. So let your actions shine out your Masonry. Let the main sermon of your life be illustrated by your conduct, and it shall not fail to be illustrious.

ANONYMOUS

In the beginning God created the Heaven and the earth.
And the earth was without form, and void;
And darkness was upon the face of the deep.
And the spirit of God moved upon the face of the waters.
And God said, "Let there be light."
And there was light.

GENESIS I:I-3

Ye are the light of the world.
A city that is set upon a hill cannot be hid.
Neither do men light a candle, and put it under a bushel,
But on a candlestick:
And it giveth light unto all that are in the house.
Let your light so shine before men,
That they will see your good works,
And glorify your Father which is in Heaven.

ST. MATTHEW 5:14-16

God has by no means settled down to rest after the well-known fabled six days of creation. He is, rather, continuously active as on the first day. To put this clumsy world together out of simple elements and let it revolve year in, year out, in the rays of the sun would certainly not have diverted Him if He had not the plan to fashion, on this material basis, a nursery for a world of spirits. Thus He is now ceaselessly active in the minds of higher endowment, in order to develop those of more limited range.

JOHANN WOLFGANG VON GOETHE

ENTERED—THE LIGHT

The way was dark, no light could I discern—
   I knew not whither, east or west, I went;
I did not even know the road would turn—
   But I on seeking "light" was solely bent.

I passed the ones who guard the sacred way
   Then I was told to kneel and 'tend a prayer
To Diety, whose mighty power holds sway
   O'er all the mortals who assembled there.

And when my heart did quake with sudden fear
   That even now I might not find the light;
A soft voice whispered in my list'ning ear:
   "Fear Not!" and all misgivings took their flight.

At last I reached a place—'twas holy ground;
   I knelt before the "Master" on the throne,
While all the other mortals gathered round
   To lend their aid and see his will was done.

I humbly asked that I the light might see,
   And learn the truth as other mortals had;
And then a voice of great authority
   Rang out! I saw the light and I was glad.

F. H. SELLERY

THE HABITATION OF THE GRAND ARCHITECT

God dwells in light!
Before the ocean of unmeasured space
    Was islanded with stars serenely bright—
Reflecting back the radiance of His face,—
He dwelt above, in Heaven's immortal bliss,
Thinking into existence that which is.

God dwells in light!
Before He laid the world's foundation-stone
    High on the nothing of primeval night,
And in Heaven's centre throned th' eternal sun,
He dwelt above, beyond the far-off sky,
With Angels born of His Eternity.

God dwells in light!
And holds within the hollow of His hand
    The universe of words which gem the night,
Which, through Heaven's sea, at His divine command.
Freighted with His own smiles now sail at even,
Fearless of storms, around the sun in Heaven.

God dwells in light!
And where He dwells, there spirits also dwell,
    Who drink fresh glory from His face so bright,
As stars drink from the sun's deep golden well
Exhaustless beams, so that they never die,
And thereby show His immortality.

J. GIERLOW

THE THREE GREAT LIGHTS

The Three Great Lights will guide our steps
    Through life's uncertain way,
And bring us safe at length to see
    The bright, eternal day.

The Holy Book our fathers read
With undimmed faith, today
Make clear our sight that we may know
Its precepts to obey.

With square of virtue, try our acts
And make them meet the test;
There is no other cause that leads
To Islands of the Blest.

Between the lines that represent
The longest, shortest day,
Keep circumscribed by compasses
That we go not astray.

The Three Great Lights will guide our steps
Through life's uncertain way,
And bring us safe at length to see
The bright, eternal day.

ANONYMOUS

GOD'S FREEMASONRY

Here in a lodge of pines I sit;
The canopy thrown over it
Is heaven's own of very blue;
Due east and west its precincts lie
And always the all-seeing eye
Of summer's sun is shining through.

Its portals open to the west;
The chipmunk, grey and sober dressed,
The tyler is: You see him dodge
To challenge every new alarm:
He has no sword upon his arm
But well he guards this secret lodge.

Our Master is that giant pine
Who bends o'er us with mien divine
   To keep the lodge in order trim:
His wardens are two grey-beard birch
Who sit like elders in a church
   Or make decorous bows to him.

The deacons are two slender trees,
Who move about whene'er the breeze
   Brings orders from the Master's seat;
Our organist? Where thickest glooms
Are darkening in the pine top's plumes
   The brother winds our music beat.

Whoever knocks upon the door
To learn the ancient wildwood lore,
   That one he is our candidate:
We strip him of his city gear,
And meet him on the level here,
   Then to our ways initiate.

We slip the hoodwink from his eye
And bid him look on earth and sky
   To read the hieroglyphics there;
More ancient these than Golden Fleece
Or Roman Eagle, Tyre, or Greece,
   Or Egypt old beyond compare.

On grass and stone and flower and sod
Is written down by hand of God
   The secrets of this Masonry;
Who has the hoodwink from his eyes
May in these common things surprise
   The awful signs of Deity.

Here bird and plant and man and beast
Are seeking their Eternal East:
   And here in springtime may be heard,
By him who doth such teachings seek
With praying heart, and wise, and meek,
   The thundering of the old Lost Word.

All things that in creation are
From smallest fly to largest star,
   In this fellowship may be
For all that floweth out from Him,
From dust to man and seraphim
   Belong to God's freemasonry.

H. L. HAYWOOD

THE INNER LIGHT

He that has light within his own clear breast
May sit i' the centre, and enjoy bright day:
But he that hides a dark soul and foul thoughts
Benighted walks under the midday sun;
Himself is his own dungeon.

JOHN MILTON

CREDO

I cannot find my way: there is no star
In all the shrouded heavens anywhere;
And there is not a whisper in the air
Of any living voice but one so far
That I can hear it only as a bar
Of lost, imperial music, played when fair
And angel fingers wove, and unaware,
Dead leaves to garlands where no roses are.

No, there is not a glimmer, nor a call,
For one that welcomes, welcomes when he fears,
The black and awful chaos of the night;
But through it all,—above, beyond it all—
I know the far-sent message of the years,
I feel the coming glory of the Light!

EDWARD ARLINGTON ROBINSON

LET THERE BE LIGHT

Let there be light, th' Almighty spoke—
Refulgent streams from chaos broke
   T' illume the rising earth;
Well pleased the Great Jehovah stood—
The Power Supreme pronounced it good,
   And gave the planets birth.
In choral numbers, Masons, join,
To bless and praise this Light divine!

Parent of Light, accept our praise,
Who shed'st on us thy brightest rays,
   The light that fills the mind!
By choice selected, lo! we stand,
By friendship joined, a social band,
   That love to aid mankind!
In choral numbers, Masons, join,
To bless and praise this Light divine!

The widow's tear, the orphan's cry,
All wants our ready hands supply,
   As far as power is given;
The naked clothe, the prisoner free—
These are thy works, sweet Charity,
   Revealed to us from heaven.
In choral numbers, Masons, join,
To bless and praise this Light divine!

THOMAS SMITH WEBB

"LET THERE BE LIGHT!"

Brother, kneel before the altar,
   In silence grave.
Show no weakness. Do not falter
   Like cowan knave.
Honest brethren stand around you,
   With heart and hand,
Ready to encourage, aid you,
   A noble band.

Here you need not fear deception—
  All are true—
Every brother here assembled
  Knelt like you.
With throbbing hearts they silent listen
  To your voice,
As you tell in earnest whisper,
  Your free choice.
Gently loose the new made brother
  From his cord,
He is bound by stronger fetters,
  On God's Word.
Hearken to the Master's language:
  "Pray for Light,"
Responsive voices chant the echo:
  "Let there be Light,"
Welcome, brother, to our household,
  You are Free;
May it ever prove a blessing
  Unto thee.

CUMMINGS

The hero is one who kindles a great light in the world, who sets up blazing torches in the dark streets of life for men to see by. The saint is the man who walks through the dark paths of the world, himself a "light."

FELIX ADLER

THE KINGDOM OF MAN

What of the outer drear,
  As long as there's inner light;
As long as the sun of cheer
  Shines ardently bright?

As long as the soul's a-wing,
  As long as the heart is true,
What power hath trouble to bring
  A sorrow to you?

26

No bar can encage the soul,
  Nor capture the spirit free,
As long as old earth shall roll,
  Or hours shall be.

Our world is the world within,
  Our life is the thought we take,
And never an outer sin
  Can mar it or break.

Brood not on the rich man's land,
  Sigh not for miser's gold,
Holding in reach of your hand
  The treasure untold.

That lies in the Mines of Heart,
  That rests in the soul alone—
Bid worry and care depart,
  Come into your own!

JOHN KENDRICK BANGS

May God grant further aid and light to keep us from standing in our own way. May He allow us to do our proper task from morning to evening and give us clear conceptions of the consequences of things. Not to be like people who complain all day about headaches and use headache remedies and then in the evening drink too much wine. May the idea of purity, extending even to the bite I put in my mouth, become ever brighter within me.

JOHANN WOLFGANG VON GOETHE

GIVE US THY LIGHT

Our God and Father of us all
Thy wondrous works are good to see
Though fortune's tides may rise and fall
Our faith and trust abide with Thee.

Oh grant us wisdom from on high
That we may live a life of worth
And give us strength to strive and try
To do Thy will while here on earth.

If from Thy chosen path we stray
Direct us to the road that's straight
Illume the lane and clear the way
Protect us from misfortune's fate.

Yet one more wish, our closing prayer
Be Thou our guide on darkest night
Teach us to live to love and share
Oh God of Grace, give us Thy Light!

ABRAHAM PELT

CLEAR THE WAY

Men of thought! be up and stirring,
   Night and day;
Sow the seed, withdraw the curtain,
   Clear the way!
Men of action, aid and cheer them,
   As ye may!
There's a fount about to stream,
There's a light about to gleam,
There's a warmth about to glow,
There's a flower about to blow;
There's midnight blackness changing
   Into grey!
Men of thought and men of action,
   Clear the way!

Once the welcome light has broken,
   Who shall say
What the unimagined glories
   Of the day?
What the evil that shall perish
   In its ray?

Aid it, hopes of honest men;
Aid the dawning, tongue and pen;
Aid it, paper, aid it, type,
Aid it, for the hour is ripe;
And our earnest must not slacken
    Into play.
Men of thought and men of action,
    Clear the way!

Lo! a cloud's about to vanish
    From the day;
And a brazen wrong to crumble
    Into clay!
With the Right shall many more
Enter, smiling at the door;
With the giant Wrong shall fall
Many others great and small,
That for ages long have held us
    For their prey.
Men of thought and men of action,
    Clear the way!

CHARLES MACKAY

BIOGRAPHY

We need no prophet's radiant phrase to know
God's greatness dwarfs the panoply of space.
His glory dims the sun's candescent glow.
In golden lines the stars and planets trace
Their shining paeans of majestic praise.
The leash of countless tides within His hand
And harmony in heaven's jewelled maze
Reveal His thoughts outnumber grains of sand.

The slow unfolding of the flower of time
Proclaims the patience of redemptive force.
From molecule to man, life's constant climb
Pays tribute to the Guide who steers the course.
He gleams in aspiration and the goal
And in the spark which lights each human soul.

GAIL BROOK BURKET

EVENTUAL LIGHT

Could not the Great Creator at one word
Have summoned complex life from steaming slime?
Omnipotence was His. Yet He preferred
The slow evolving, many-eoned climb
From molecule to man. Could He not kill
The serpent troubling Eden, if He would?
All-wise He gave men freedom of the will
That they might find their way to brotherhood.

Then why should we despair, if we ascend
With fumbling steps? We shall achieve our goal.
From clan to nation to one world will end
As God intended, when He gave man soul.
With confidence we grope through darkest night,
For we are certain of eventual light.

GAIL BROOK BURKET

LIGHT SHINING OUT OF DARKNESS

God moves in a mysterious way,
    His wonders to perform;
He plants His footsteps in the sea,
    And rides upon the storm.

Deep in unfathomable mines
    Of never-failing skill
He treasures up His bright designs.
    And works His sovereign will.

Ye fearful saints, fresh courage take;
    The clouds ye so much dread
Are big with mercy, and shall break
    In blessings on your head.

Judge not the Lord by feeble sense,
  But trust Him for His grace;
Behind a frowning Providence
  He hides a smiling face.

His purposes will ripen fast,
  Unfolding every hour;
The bud may have a bitter taste,
  But sweet will be the flower.

Blind unbelief is sure to err,
  And scan His work in vain;
God is His own interpreter,
  And He will make it plain.

WILLIAM COWPER

GRANT THY LIGHT

O God of Ages look tonight
Upon Thy Craftsman; let Thy light
Burn on the altars of his heart,
And fit him for the Mason's Art.

That light which pales the brightest star,
And leaps the void of spaces far
To crown with beauty morning sky
And evening hills to glorify—

Touch with that light his heart, and grant,
Oh God, grace to this supplicant,
That in Thy temple he may be
An ornament of Masonry.

FRANKLIN CABLE

FIAT LUX!

"Let there be light!" It is God's word.
From the beginning this was heard—
"Let there be light!" Then o'er the earth
Life's greatest blessings came to birth!

"Let there be light!" The light of Truth
Gives guidance unto age and youth.
"Let there be light!" The light of Love
Brings joy to all from God above.

"Let there be light!" At last we see
The way to true fraternity.
"Let there be light!" So shall we find
The tie which binds God and mankind!

W. J. THOMPSON

Oh Thou who hast called us out of darkness to be bearers of light; we beseech Thee to make us helpers in the world. Take away from us the love of ease, and fear of men. Show us the simple things that we can do to help our neighbours to be good. Brighten the daily round of tasks that we have undertaken and are tempted to neglect. Make us faithful to the trust that life has put upon us; hold us to the humblest duty.

Prepare our hearts in sympathy to be partners in suffering with the weak; partners in eager service with the strong.

Reveal to us the wavering ranks of those that are struggling upward that we may cheer and support our comrades unknown. Remove from us the love of glory and the thirst for praise. Give us, in weariness, refreshment, and in strength, peace; but when we are idle, send shame, and when we are false, send fear, to bring us back to Thee. By Thy Love restrain our censorious speech and teach us to commend. By Thy Wisdom enlighten our plans, and direct our endeavours for the common wealth. And give to us the vision of that bright City of God upon earth where all shall share the best they have, in thought and deed, and none shall harm or make afraid.

And establish Thou the work of our hands upon us; yes, the work of our hands establish Thou it.

ANONYMOUS

LIGHT

The pathway of man through the ages wends
From the darkness that enveloped the past
His guiding star that ray of hope
Whose brilliance shall eternally last.

Obscured at times by the fog and mists
Of forces allegedly real
Yet onward he goes, ever seeking the truth
That truth which he knows will heal.

The bruised and the broken, the sorrowful, sad,
Who seem lost in the mist in the way,
Feel the touch of that unseen gentle hand
And reverently kneel to pray.

The light of truth floods the thought of the man
And joy wells up in his heart,
For he's found that the source of that light is God
And he vows from it never to part.

EVART EMERSON OVERTON

LIGHT, MORE LIGHT

Your first great need, O Brother mine,
        Is Light,
To know the glow in which you live,
        And love:
The ills of life are only dreams
        Of night—
Face but the glorious Light which shines
        Above.

Your second need is still more Light—
    Nor dream
On lofty peaks alone to see
    Its flood;
For down the vale of Brotherhood
    Its gleam
In glory fills the darkened world
    With good.

At last, with long and steadfast gaze
    On Light,
You'll lose the phantom dreams of night—
    Nor e'er
Recall these unrealities
    Of night,
For Light of God's eternal day
    Is fair.

ULYSSES F. AXTELL

THE LIGHT IN THE TEMPLE

In the ancient days of story,
  When the fathers sought the light,
And the temple's golden glory
  Blazed on old Moriah's height;
Deep within the sacred portals
  Of that holy house of prayer,
Thrilling awed and trembling mortals,
  Burned a mystic brightness there.

Day and night its glow extended
  Thru the calm religious gloom,
While the long-robed priests attended
  In the consecrated room.
'Twas the pure Shekinah gleaming,—
  Symbol of the eternal God,
As His light, 'mid darkness beaming,
  Dwells within the human clod.

34

Tell me, brother, as you travel
　　On the rugged earthly way,
Should the Master Builder's gavel
　　Sound your final call today;
As your weary feet are turning
　　At the summons to depart,
Can you find the God-light burning
　　In the temple of your heart?

Could you find the clear rays brightly
　　Showing a record called "Well done,"—
Telling good deeds wrought uprightly,
　　Battles fought and victories won?
Has the pure divine example
　　Been for you the better part,
Safely lodged within the temple
　　Of a true Masonic heart?

Let your willing hands be doing
　　Daily for a brother's needs,
Thus the sacred flame renewing
　　With the oil of kindly deeds.
Keep your temple swept and garnished
　　With your tenets' rule divine,
And your light, its ray untarnished,
　　Thru the night will ever shine.

CARL W. MASON

The Builders

MAN—THE BUILDER

Man has always been a builder, and nowhere has he shown himself more significantly than in the buildings he has created. When we stand before them—whether it be a mud hut, the house of a cliff-dweller stuck like the nest of a swallow on the side on a canyon, a Pyramid, a Parthenon, or a Pantheon—we seem to read into his soul. The builder may have gone, perhaps ages before, but here he has left something of himself, his hopes, his fears, his ideas, his dreams. Even in the remote recesses of the Andes, amidst the riot of nature, and where man is now a mere savage, we come upon the remains of vast, vanished civilizations, where art and science and religion reached unknown heights. Wherever humanity has lived and wrought, we find the crumbling remains of towers, temples, and tombs, monuments of its industry and its aspiration. Also, whatever else man may have been—cruel, tyrannous, vindictive—his buildings always have a reference to religion. They bespeak a vivid sense of the Unseen and his awareness to it. Of a truth, the story of the Tower of Babel is more than a myth. Man has ever been trying to build to heaven, embodying his prayer and his dream in brick and stone.

Here, then, are the real foundations of Masonry, both material and moral: in the deep need and aspiration of man, and his creative impulse; in his instinctive faith, his quest of the Ideal, and his love of the Light. Underneath all his building lay the feeling, prophetic of his last and highest thought, that the earthly house of his life should be in right relation with its heavenly prototype, the world-temple —imitating on earth the house not made with hands, eternal in the heavens. And as he wrought his faith and dream into reality, it was but natural that the tools of the builder should become emblems of the thought of the thinker. Not only his tools, but, the very stones with which he worked became sacred symbols—the temple itself a vision of that House of Doctrine, that Home of the Soul, which, though unseen, he is building in the midst of the years.

JOSEPH FORT NEWTON

MAN-MAKING

We are blind until we see
That in the human plan
Nothing is worth the making if
It does not make the man.

Why build these cities glorious
If man unbuilded goes?
In vain we build the work unless
The builder also grows.

EDWIN MARKHAM

SERVICE

Therefore when we build, let us think that we build forever. Let it not be for the present delight, nor for the present use alone. Let it be such work as our descendants will thank us for, and let us think as we lay stone on stone, that the time is to come when those stones will be held sacred because our hands have touched them, and that men will say as they look upon the labour and wrought substance of them, "See what our fathers did for us."

JOHN RUSKIN

THE BUILDERS

All are architects of Fate,
   Working in these walls of Time;
Some with massive deeds and great,
   Some with ornaments of rhyme.

Nothing useless is, or low;
   Each thing in its place is best;
And what seems but idle show
   Strengthens and supports the rest.

For the structure that we raise,
   Time is with materials filled;
Our to-days and yesterdays
   Are the blocks with which we build.

Truly shape and fashion these;
   Leave no yawning gaps between;
Think not, because no man sees,
   Such things will remain unseen.

In the elder days of Art,
   Builders wrought with greatest care
Each minute and unseen part;
   For the Gods see everywhere.

Let us do our work as well,
   Both the unseen and the seen;
Make the house, where Gods may dwell,
   Beautiful, entire, and clean.

Else our lives are incomplete,
   Standing in these walls of Time,
Broken stairways, where the feet
   Stumble as they seek to climb.

Build to-day, then, strong and sure,
   With a firm and ample base,
And ascending and secure
   Shall to-morrow find its place.

Thus alone can we attain
To those turrets, where the eye
Sees the world as one vast plain,
And one boundless reach of sky.

HENRY WADSWORTH LONGFELLOW

THE BUILDERS

If in the rearing of an edifice
　We form one stone that makes the perfect whole;
To us 'twould be the beau-ideal of bliss
　And prove glad unction to the work-worn soul.
A Temple with proportions just and true
　Can but erected be by Masons skilled,
Instructed by an Architect who knew
　Exactly how to tell them what to build.
And he taught us—however small the stone—
　To plumb and level by th' unerring Square—
To make it pattern, so that all might own
　'Twas strong and beautiful beyond compare,—
With Chisel and with Gavel we have wrought
　To gain "Well Done,"—The Tongue of Good Report.

CHARLES F. FORSHAW

Now! Tell me about your church. . . .

It has to be seen in a certain way, under certain conditions. Some people never *see* it at all. You must understand, this is no dead pile of stones and unmeaning timber. *It is a living thing.* . . . When you enter it you hear a sound—a sound as of some mighty poem chanted. Listen long enough, and you will learn it is made up of the beating of human hearts, of the nameless music of men's souls—that is, if you have ears. If you have eyes, you will presently see the church itself—a looming mystery of many shapes and shadows, leaping sheer from floor to dome. The work of no ordinary builder! . . . The pillars of it go up like the brawny trunks of heroes: the sweet human flesh of men and women is moulded about its bulwarks, strong, impregnable: the faces of little children laugh out from every corner-stone: the terrible spans and arches of it are the joined hands of comrades; and up in the heights and spaces there are inscribed the numberless musings of all

39

the dreamers of the world. It is yet building—building and built upon. Sometimes the work goes forward in deep darkness: sometimes in blinding light: now beneath the burden of unutterable anguish: now to the tune of a great laughter and heroic shoutings like the cry of thunder. Sometimes, in the silence of the night-time, one may hear the tiny hammerings of the comrades at work up in the dome—the comrades that have climbed ahead.

CHARLES RANN KENNEDY

A BAG OF TOOLS

Isn't it strange
That princes and kings,
And clowns that caper
In sawdust rings,
And common people
Like you and me
Are builders for eternity?

Each is given a bag of tools,
A shapeless mass,
A book of rules;
And each must make—
Ere life is flown—
A stumbling block
Or a stepping stone.

R. L. SHARPE

WORK

A Song of Triumph

Work!
Thank God for the might of it,
The ardour, the urge, the delight of it—
Work that springs from the heart's desire,
Setting the brain and the soul on fire—
Oh, what is so good as the heat of it,
And what is so glad as the beat of it,
And what is so kind as the stern command,
Challenging brain and heart and hand?

Work!
Thank God for the pride of it,
For the beautiful, conquering tide of it,
Sweeping the life in its furious flood,
Thrilling the arteries, cleansing the blood,
Mastering stupor and dull despair,
Moving the dreamer to do and dare.
Oh, what is so good as the urge of it,
And what is so glad as the surge of it,
And what is so strong as the summons deep,
Rousing the torpid soul from sleep?

Work!
Thank God for the pace of it,
For the terrible, keen, swift race of it;
Fiery steeds in full control,
Nostrils a-quiver to greet the goal.
Work, the Power that drives behind,
Guiding the purposes, taming the mind,
Holding the runaway wishes back,
Reining the will to one steady track,
Speeding the energies faster, faster,
Triumphing over disaster.
Oh, what is so good as the pain of it,
And what is so great as the gain of it?
And what is so kind as the cruel goad,
Forcing us on through the rugged road?

Work!
Thank God for the swing of it,
For the clamouring, hammering ring of it,
Passion and labour daily hurled
On the mighty anvils of the world.
Oh, what is so fierce as the flame of it?
And what is so huge as the aim of it?
Thundering on through dearth and doubt,
Calling the plan of the Maker out.
Work, the Titan; Work, the friend,
Shaping the earth to a glorious end,
Draining the swamps and blasting the hills,
Doing whatever the Spirit wills—

Rending a continent apart,
To answer the dream of the Master heart.
Thank God for a world where none may shirk—
Thank God for the splendour of work!

ANGELA MORGAN

I pray you with all earnestness to prove and to know within your
hearts that all things lovely and righteous are possible for those who
believe in their possibility, and who determine that for their part they
will make each day's work contribute to them. Let every dawn of
morning be to you as the beginning of life, and every setting sun be
to you as its close. Then let every one of these short lives leave its
sure record of some kindly thing done for others, some goodly
strength or knowledge gained for yourselves. So, from day to day and
strength to strength, you shall build up an edifice of which it shall not
be said, "See what manner of stones are here," but *see what manner of
men.*"

JOHN RUSKIN

THE BRIDGE BUILDER

An old man, going a lone highway,
Came at the evening, cold and grey,
To a chasm, vast and deep and wide,
Through which was flowing a sullen tide.
The old man crossed in the twilight dim—
That sullen stream had no fears for him;
But he turned, when he reached the other side,
And built a bridge to span the tide.

"Old man," said a fellow pilgrim near,
"You are wasting strength in building here.
Your journey will end with the ending day;
You never again must pass this way.
You have crossed the chasm, deep and wide,
Why build you the bridge at the eventide?"

The builder lifted his old grey head.
"Good friend, in the path I have come," he said,
"There followeth after me today
A youth whose feet must pass this way.
This chasm that has been naught to me
To that fair-haired youth may a pitfall be.
He, too, must cross in the twilight dim;
Good friend, I am building the bridge for *him*."

WILL ALLEN DROMGOOLE

THE TROWEL

The tools of a true Master Mason—
  A man who has proven his skill—
Are any or all as he chooses,
  His tasks to correctly fulfil.
Foremost of these is the Trowel,
  Which practical builders all class
As the tool for the spreading of mortar
  Uniting the house in one mass.

But we as Freemasons would use it
  For purpose more noble and grand,
As Craftsmen have faithfully taught us,
  As Masonry's rituals command,
To spread the cement of affection,
  Devotion and brotherly love,
To bring peace, good will and contentment
  On earth as in Heaven above.

Yea; that's the cement that unites us
  In one sacred union of friends—
Brothers 'mongst whom no contention,
  Nor discord nor diff'rence portends,
Except that most noble contention
  By Masons Accepted and Free;
Or rather that fine emulation
  Of who can best work and agree.

MICHAEL N. SALMORE

43

ORDER AND THE BEES

Therefore doth heaven divide
The state of man in divers functions,
Setting endeavour in continual motion;
To which is fixéd, as an aim or butt,
Obedience: for so work the honey-bees,
Creatures that by a rule in nature teach
The act of order to a peopled kingdom.
They have a king and officers of sorts;
Where some, like magistrates, correct at home,
Others, like merchants, venture trade abroad,
Others, like soldiers, arméd in their stings,
Make boot upon the summer's velvet buds;
Which pillage they with merry march bring home
To the tent-royal of their emperor:
Who, busied in his majesty, surveys
The singing masons building roofs of gold,
The civil citizens kneading up the honey,
The poor mechanic porters crowding in
Their heavy burdens at his narrow gate,
The sad-eyed justice, with his surly hum,
Delivering o'er to executors pale
The lazy yawning drone. I this infer,
That many things, having full reference
To one consent, may work contrariously.

WILLIAM SHAKESPEARE

THE MASON'S HOLY HOUSE

We have a Holy House to build,
    A Temple splendid and divine,
To be with glorious memories filled;
    Of Right and Truth to be the shrine.
How shall we build it strong and fair,—
This Holy House of Praise and Prayer,
Firm-set and solid, grandly great?
How shall we all its rooms prepare
    For use, for ornament, for state?

Our God hath given the wood and stone,
    And we must fashion them aright,
Like those who toiled on Lebanon,
    Making the labour their delight:
This House, this Palace, this God's Home,
This Temple with its lofty dome,
    Must be in all proportions fit,
That heavenly messengers may come
    To lodge with those who tenant it.

Build squarely up the stately walls,
    The two symbolic columns raise,
And let the lofty courts and halls
With all their golden glories blaze.
There, in the Kadosh-Kadoshim,
Between the broad-winged cherubim,
    Where the Shekinah once abode,
The heart shall raise its daily hymn
    Of gratitude and love to God.

ALBERT PIKE

THE BUILDERS

Here are bricks and there is mortar for ye, build—
Build houses, castles, sanctuaries,
    And idols for your joy.
There's colour, and there is gold for ye to gild
Your palaces, your statuary;
    And Time will all destroy.

There is toil, and there is sorrow for ye, build—
Build cares, fears, and anxiety,
    Till Death takes ye away.
There are foes in hate and jealousy so skill'd,
Can tarnish fame and glitterings,
    And you'll have nought to say.

Here is truth, and there is wisdom for ye, build—
Build kindness, virtue, charity,
   And for such works you may
Depend that there is much space which may be fill'd
With greater, stronger monuments
   Than Time can wash away.

There is love, and there is mercy for ye, build—
Build holiness and righteousness
   Till one continual day.
There have peace and everlasting life been will'd,
Eternal glory, happiness,
   To those who build this way.

LOUIS DE VILLE

THE CORNERSTONE

We have laid the stone all truly with a Master Craftsman's care,
We have tested it and tried it by the level, plumb and square,
We've made a firm foundation for our children's children's toil
And empty poured the vessels of their corn and wine and oil.

What further is remaining save stone on stone to rear
That soon the finished building in its glory shall appear?
What more to do than giving to this pile its latest touch?
And a Voice that stirs the stillness makes this answer, "There is
   much."

"There is work to do, my brothers, wrought of neither stone nor
   steel
And never dome nor tower can its majesty reveal,
For this, the nobler labour, ere his toil can make it whole,
Must be performed in darkness in the Master Craftsman's soul.

"There are works of loving-kindness and of charity and good
And a structure to be builded with the stones of brotherhood,
For this mighty Temple's fabric is an empty mocking shell
Unless within it there be built a shrine of souls as well.

46

'Take heed, then, Master Craftsmen, when this Temple shall arise
With its brave and gleaming towers pointing grandly to the skies.
Let yourselves compose the structure, let yourselves the Temple be,
That shall stand in great proportion unto all Eternity."

R. J. MCLAUCHLIN

DO IT NOW!

If you've got a job to do,
                    Do it now!
If it's one you wish were through,
                    Do it now!
If you're sure the job's your own,
Do not hem and haw and groan—
                    Do it now!
Don't put off a bit of work,
                    Do it now!
It doesn't pay to shirk,
                    Do it now!
If you want to fill a place
And be useful to the race,
Just get up and take a brace—
                    Do it now!
Don't linger by the way,
                    Do it now!

ANONYMOUS

The ambitions of great men, the suspicions of little men, the constant misunderstanding of all men, may undermine any structure that this generation builds. If, however, we build with wisdom, and with courage, and with patience, those that come after us will be helped by our work. Our building may fall, but if we have built aright, some of the foundation stones will remain and become part of the structure that will ultimately abide.

DWIGHT MORROW

BUILDERS ARE WE

Builders of walls are we, and labour to fashion a temple,
Each has some part assigned, one stone to his hands is entrusted;
Simple the work may seem, unworthy the skill of an artist,
Yet in the Builder's plan the humblest of tasks is momentous.

Lacking the keystone wedge the arch must collapse into ruin,
Take from the arc one block the key can no longer secure it.
This is the changeless law, that each lend support to his fellows,
And in return shall each, upheld by his comrades, stand dauntless.

Slender, and staunch, and tall, uprises the spire o'er the city—
Symbol of God's own hand inscribing His name on the heavens—
Still it could never stand reflecting the noonday effulgence
But for the stones unseen deep hid in the temple's foundation.

Stones in a wall are we, and each to its fellows essential,
Each has his niche assigned, none other can fill his place for him;
Say not There is no worth in this simple part I am given,
For in the Builder's sight the humblest of tasks is of import.

GEORGE H. FREE

THE TROWEL

Now each man builds a Temple by his single strength alone,
And whatsoe'er its worthiness, that Temple is his own,
Of chaste and gleaming marble or of ugly mud and clay,
Each Temple must its builder's self, his secret soul, display.

The world beholds and reasons "Lo, this builder's house is fair;
All honour to the Craftsman who has set such beauty there;
For such a noble monument, so straight and white and grand,
Reveals a wise and cleanly brain, a strong and cleanly hand."

But oftentimes it happens that, ere many years have sped,
This Temple's symmetry departs, its beauty wholly fled,
And what was once magnificence is soil and wrack and rust,
And perfect columns find their rest in overwhelming dust.

Ah, world, look closely when you would a Temple well discern,
And peradventure lessons may you profitably learn,
Behold its stones but ere you say "The hand that wrought was
    clean."
Take heed of other buildings and remark what lies between.

There is no house the Master sees—and calls the builder good—
Whose stones are not anointed by the hand of brotherhood,
Which have not felt the Trowel's touch which there the mortar
    laid,
The mortar that the builder's self, his secret soul, displayed.

Howe'er so great the Temple's grace, whate'er the builder's pain,
Because it lacked the Trowel's touch, the same was reared in vain,
And in despite of outward strength, of beauty or renown,
Because it lacked the Trowel's touch, the same shall crumble
    down.

For each man builds a Temple by his single might alone,
And whatsoe'er its worthiness, that Temple is his own;
The world may judge the beauty which the world's blind eyes
    have seen,
But only may the Master say "The builder's hand was clean."

R. J. MCLAUCHLIN

THE DAY AND THE WORK

To each man is given a day and his work for the day;
And once, and no more, he is given to travel this way.
And woe if he flies from the task, whatever the odds;
For the task is appointed to him on the scroll of the gods.

There is waiting a work where only his hands can avail;
And so, if he falters, a chord in the music will fail.
He may laugh to the sky, he may lie for an hour in the sun;
But he dare not go hence till the labour appointed is done.

49

To each man is given a marble to carve for the wall;
A stone that is needed to heighten the beauty of all;
And only his soul has the magic to give it a grace;
And only his hands have the cunning to put it in place.

We are given one hour to parley and struggle with Fate,
Our wild hearts filled with the dream, our brains with the high
    debate.
It is given to look on life once, and once only to die:
One testing, and then at a sign we go out of this sky.

Yes, the task that is given to each man, no other can do;
So the errand is waiting; it has waited through ages for you.
And now you appear; and the Hushed Ones are turning their
    gaze
To see what you do with your chance in the chamber of days.

EDWIN MARKHAM

"What are you doing?" a man asked three labourers beside a building
under construction.
    The first man replied, "Stone-cuttin'."
    The second smiled. "Puttin' in time—until a better job comes
along."
    The third man waited a moment and then said simply, "I'm building
a cathedral!"

ANONYMOUS

QUIET WORK

One lesson, Nature, let me learn from thee,
One lesson which in every wind is blown,
One lesson of two duties kept at one
Though the loud world proclaim their enmity—
Of toil unsevered from tranquillity;
Of labour, that in lasting fruit outgrows
Far noisier schemes, accomplished in repose,
Too great for haste, too high for rivalry.

Yes, while on earth a thousand discords ring,
Man's fitful uproar mingling with his toil,
Still do thy sleepless ministers move on,
Their glorious tasks in silence perfecting;
Still working, blaming still our vain turmoil;
Labourers that shall not fail, when man is gone.

MATTHEW ARNOLD

ODE

We are the music-makers,
  And we are the dreamers of dreams,
Wandering by lone sea-breakers,
  And sitting by desolate streams;
World-losers and world-forsakers,
  On whom the pale moon gleams:
Yet we are the movers and shakers
  Of the world for ever, it seems.

With wonderful deathless ditties
We build up the world's great cities,
  And out of a fabulous story
  We fashion an empire's glory:
One man with a dream, at pleasure,
  Shall go forth and conquer a crown;
And three with a new song's measure
  Can trample a kingdom down.

We, in the ages lying
  In the buried past of the earth,
Built Nineveh with our sighing,
  And Babel itself with our mirth;
And o'erthrew them with prophesying
  To the old of the new world's worth;
For each age is a dream that is dying,
  Or one that is coming to birth.

ARTHUR WILLIAM O'SHAUGHNESSY

EARTH IS ENOUGH

We men of earth have here the stuff
Of Paradise—we have enough!
We need no other stones to build
The stairs into the unfulfilled,—
No other ivory for the doors—
No other marble for the floors—
No other cedar for the beam
And dome of man's immortal dream.

Here on the paths of every day—
Here on the common human way
Is all the stuff the gods would take
To build a Heaven, to mould and make
New Edens. Ours the stuff sublime
To build Eternity in time!

EDWIN MARKHAM

That Masons are builders can be seen by the name . . .By teaching men the doctrines of temperance, fortitude, prudence and justice, together with the many lessons drawn from, and daily application to the activities of life, deep foundations are laid upon which loftiest character must stand. When brotherly love, relief and truth really enter into the fibre of a man's being, there is little room for the selfish and the debased. His instincts and his aspirations are toward the uplift that comes from a joyful service to mankind. That

I AM MY BROTHER'S KEEPER

is demonstrated in every avenue of life whether I am ready to concede it or not . . . Service and sacrifice are the crucible in which the base metals of greed, avarice, and selfishness are left as the dross of life. If thy brother would have thee go with him one mile, that is thy duty. When to this is added gladly, a second mile, that is a blessed privilege. Masonry puts into a man's breast

THE SWEET SERVICE OF THE SECOND MILE

Masonry's mission, therefore, to the individual is to uplift his character and establish a nobler manhood.

OWEN SCOTT

LOSE THE DAY LOITERING

Lose the day loitering, 'twill be the same story
To-morrow, and the next more dilatory,
For indecision brings its own delays,
And days are lost lamenting o'er lost days.
Are you in earnest? Seize this very minute!
What you can do, or think you can, begin it!
Only engage, and then the mind grows heated;
Begin it, and the work will be completed.

JOHANN WOLFGANG VON GOETHE

BEEHIVE

Industrious Application

A society whose motto is, "Travel and travail, walk and work," sees practical suggestions to duty in the beehive. Well said the poet, "To do nothing, is to serve the devil and transgress the law of God."

None idle here! look where you will, they all
Are active, all engaged in meet pursuit;
Not happy else. No, for the Master's voice
That called them first, is ringing in their ears;
Go build! go build! a brief six days of toil
I have allotted, arduous toil, but brief;
The burden and the heat ye must endure
All uncomplainingly,—such is my will,
In darksome quarry, and on toilsome mount,
And heated wall;—go build! not happy else!

ROBERT MORRIS

MASON MARKS

They're traced in lines on the Parthenon,
    Inscribed by the subtle Greek;
And Roman legions have carved them on
    Walls, roads and arch antique;

Long ere the Goth, with vandal hand,
    Gave scope to his envy dark,
The Mason craft in many a land
    Has graven its Mason mark.

The obelisk old and the pyramids,
    Around which a mystery clings,—
The hieroglyphs on the coffin lids
    Of weird Egyptian kings,—
Syria, Carthage and Pompeii
    Buried and strewn and stark,
Have marble records that will not die,
    Their primitive Mason mark.

Upon column and frieze and capital,
    In the eye of the chaste volute,—
On Scotia's curve, or an astrogal,
    Or in triglyp's channel acute,—
Cut somewhere on the entablature,
    And oft, like a sudden spark,
Flashing a light on a date obscure,
    Shines many a Mason mark.

These craftsmen old had a genial whim,
    That nothing could e'er destroy,
With a love of their art that naught could dim,
    They toiled with a chronic joy;
Nothing was too complex to essay,
    In aught they dashed to embark;
They triumphed on many an Appian Way,
    Where they'd left their Mason mark.

Crossing the Alps like Hannibal,
    Or skirting the Pyrenees,
On peak and plain, in crypt and cell,
    On foot or on bandaged knees;—
From Tiber to Danube, from Rhine to Seine,
    They needed no "letters of marque";—
Their art was their passport in France and Spain,
    And in Britain their Mason mark.

The monolith grey and Druid chair,
  The pillars and towers of Gael,
In Ogham occult their age they bear,
  That time can only reveal.
Live on, old monuments of the past,
  Our beacons through ages dark!
In primal majesty still you'll last,
  Endeared by each Mason mark.

ANONYMOUS

THE TRAINERS

My name is Trouble—I'm a busy bloke—
  I am the test of Courage—and of Class—
I bind the coward to a bitter yoke,
  I drive the craven from the crowning pass;
Weaklings I crush before they come to fame;
  But as the red star guides across the night,
I train the stalwart for a better game;
  I drive the brave into a harder fight.

My name is Hard Luck—the wrecker of rare dreams—
  I follow all who seek the open fray;
I am the shadow where the far light gleams
  For those who seek to know the open way;
Quitters I break before they reach the crest,
  But where the red field echoes with the drums,
I build the fighter for the final test
  And mould the brave for any drive that comes.

My name is Sorrow—I shall come to all
  To block the surfeit of an endless joy;
Along the Sable Road I pay my call
  Before the sweetness of success can cloy;
And weaker souls shall weep amid the throng
  And fall before me, broken and dismayed;
But braver hearts shall know that I belong
  And take me in, serene and unafraid.

My name's Defeat—but through the bitter fight,
    To those who know, I'm something more than friend;
For I can build beyond the wrath of might
    And drive away all yellow from the blend;
For those who quit, I am the final blow,
    But for the brave who seek their chance to learn,
I show the way, at last, beyond the foe,
    To where the scarlet flames of triumph burn.

GRANTLAND RICE

FATHER'S LODGE

Father's lodge, I well remember, wasn't large as lodges go;
There was trouble in December getting to it through the snow.
But he seldom missed a meeting; drifts or blossoms in the lane,
Still the Tyler heard his greetings, winter ice or summer rain.

Father's lodge thought nothing of it: 'mid their labours and their
    cares
Those old Masons learned to love it, that fraternity of theirs.
What's a bit of stormy weather, when a little down the road
Men are gathering together, helping bear each other's load?

Father's lodge had made a village: men of father's sturdy brawn
Turned a wilderness to tillage, seized the flag, and carried on,
Made a village, built a city, shaped a county, formed a state,
Simple men, not wise nor witty—humble men, and yet how
    great!

Father's lodge had caught the gleaming of the great Masonic past;
Thinking, toiling, daring, dreaming, they were builders to the last.
Quiet men, not rich nor clever, with the tools they found at hand
Building for the great forever, first a village then a land.

Father's lodge no temple builded shaped of steel and carved of
    stone;
Marble columns, ceilings gilded, father's lodge has never known.
But a heritage of glory they have left, the humble ones—
They have left their mighty story in the keeping of their sons.

DOUGLAS MALLOCH

GOOD DEEDS

If I could turn back the hands of time,
    And start life all over anew,
If I could have life as only mine,
    The many good deeds I would do.

First, I would build around me
    A wall of friendship true,
From those of God's people,
    The ones that I really knew.

I would have a smile for everyone,
    To start each day aright,
And cause no one a single pain,
    I would try with all my might.

My life would be guided by the Plumb,
    I would live upon the Square,
And when I left this dear old world
    I would leave no troubles there.

But I cannot turn back the hands of time
    Nor live my life anew;
But the rest of my days I can surely spend
    In seeing the good I can do.

W. A. KUNCE

ONLY A BUILDING

You may delve down to rock for your foundation piers,
You may go with your steel to the sky;
You may purchase the best of the thought of the years
And the finest of workmanship buy;
You may line with the rarest of marble each wall,
And with gold you may tint it, but then
It is only a building, if it, after all,
Isn't filled with the spirit of men.

You may put up a structure of brick and stone,
Such as never was put up before;
Place therein the costliest woods that are grown
And carve every pillar and door;
You may fill it with splendours of quarry and mine,
With the glories of brush and of pen,
But it's only a building though ever so fine,
If it hasn't the spirit of men.

You may build such a structure that lightning can't harm,
Or one that an earthquake can't raze;
You may build it of granite and boast that its charm
Shall last to the end of all days.
But you might as well never have builded at all,
Never cleared off the bog and the fen,
If after it's finished its sheltering wall
Doesn't stand for the spirit of men.

For it isn't the marble, nor is it the stone,
Nor is it the columns of steel,
By which is the worth of an edifice known,
But by something that's living and real.

EDGAR A. GUEST

THE BUILDER

I built my house on the Sands of Time,
    A house that I built to stay;
But the tide came in—as the tide will come,
    And it washed the sands away.
Then my house fell down, as a house will fall,
    And hope went out with the tide,
But I built again, as a man will build,
    If he be a man of pride.

Then came the storm with the fierce whirlwind,
   And my house was wrecked again.
And I stood and looked at my labour lost,
   And it all seemed so in vain.
But I built again in another place—
   Where the storm and the tide came not,
And I felt safe in my new strong house—
   But one thing I forgot.

It was the flames with their red-hot tongues,
   That came in the still of night,
And they ate it up—as the flames will eat,
   Though I strove with all my might.
And again I looked at the house that was,
   Then knew it was not to be,
For a well built house won't fall three times,
   When built for eternity.

Now why should I build a house three times,
   And why should it three times fall?
Were it better I built a house that falls
   Than never to build at all?
Then came a thought from the Great Somewhere,
   I had not followed the rules,
For a well built house won't fall three times,
   When built with the Master's Tools.

So I built again with the Master's Tools,
   The Level, the Plumb and the Square,
Each ashlar hewn from the Rock of Faith
   Was polished and laid with care;
And the plans I used were the Plans of Life
   And my house it faced the sun,
Now I dwell therein as a man should dwell,
   When the Craftsman's work's well done.

HERBERT N. FARRAR

THE WORK DIVINE

Conceited man, whose empty boast
    Is that thy works shall live for aye,
Behold the ruin of the host
    Who wrought like thee, but won decay!
Proud Babel's tower, vanished quite;
    The crumbling sphinx and pyramid
In vain attest their builders' might
    For e'en their names from us are hid.

No marvel that those ruins stand,
    Slow crumbling in decrepit shame;
The wonder is, though wisely planned,
    How brief indeed their builders' fame.
How puny are the deeds of man,
    When to Creation's works compared;
How transitory is their span,
    Their plan how weak, when time has bared.

Consider Him whose hand has hung
    Those orbs on high, thy steps to lead,
His sparkling stardust broadcast flung,
    Like as a sower casts his seed;
Who set the bounds for ocean's tide,
    Commanded mountains, Stand ye here,
Unrolled the boundless prairies wide,
    And fixed the seasons of the year.

Vain creature, hang thy head in shame!
    Behold the heavens' vaulted bowl;
There read thy great Creator's fame
    Inscribed upon its blazing scroll.
The firmament displays His skill,
    Through far-flung space His glories shine.
Ye proud bombastic lips be still
    Before the works of One divine!

GEORGE H. FREE

60

THE PLUMB

Build up your life like the temple of old
  With stones that are polished and true;
Cement it with love, and adorn it with gold
  As all Master builders should do:
Upon a foundation, well chosen and strong,
  Build now for the ages to come:
Make use of the good, while rejecting the wrong—
  And test all your work with the plumb.

NEAL A. MCAULAY

If one advances confidently in the direction of his dreams, and endeavours to live the life which he has imagined, he will meet with a
success unexpected in common hours . . . If you have built castles
in the air, your work need not be lost; that is where they should be.
Now put the foundations under them.

HENRY DAVID THOREAU

THE LEVEL

Oh, he who rides th' untrammelled winds of fame,
  And he whose steps are painful made and slow,
Shall reach at length one goal; yea, each the same;
  For on Time's Level do their courses go.

And man, composed of fragile mortal stuff,
  His fame must doff, his glory leave behind,
Nor pride nor power has potency enough
  To raise one mortal man above his kind.

The ages' wisdom gives this message birth,
  The sweep of generations can display
The bones of Caesar, mightiest of earth,
  Beside his vassals, crumbling in the clay.

And thus the Craftsmen anciently were taught
 That glory, on Time's Level, finds defeat,
And there have they their full communion sought,
 And there they evermore shall work and meet.

The mighty and the lowly there shall bend
 Unto the nearest tasks their lives provide;
The humble shall arise, the high descend,
 As brothers, on the Level, side by side.

R. J. MCLAUCHLIN

THE SQUARE

The elders of our ancient art
 Built Temples, high and fair,
And never stone was laid in place
And never column rose in grace,
 Untested by the Square.

Our elders left a heritage,
 Upreared in wood and stone,
That we, who follow, might behold
The craft of these, the men of old,
 Thus, through their works, made known.

Oh, let us do our work as well,
 Though never dome we raise,
With brain untutored, hand unskilled,
A square-set Temple may we build,
 Of simple nights and days.

The Square of Virtue for our acts
 Wherewith to set them true,
Can make a building, standing quite
As worthy in our children's sight,
 And in the Master's, too.

62

Thus may we, too, great builders be
  As any ancient race;
Our Temple is the square-set mind,
Wherein the Master's Self may find
  A fitting dwelling-place.

R. J. McLAUCHLIN

BUILDING

Brick by brick the Masons builded
Till the highest cross was gilded
  With the glory of the sun,
  Till the noble task was done.
  Step by step and one by one
Wall and rafter, roof and spire
Men were lifting ever higher,
  Not in some mysterious way—
With the tasks of every day.

Architects may do their dreaming,
See their visioned turrets gleaming
  High above them in the skies;
  Yet the wisdom of the wise
  Cannot make one roof arise—
Hearts must sing and hands must labour,
Man must work beside his neighbour,
  Brick on brick and toil on toil
  Building upward from the soil.

So we build a lodge or nation,
On the firmly fixed foundation
  Of a flag or craft or creed;
  But on top of that we need
  Many a noble thought and deed,
Day by day and all the seven,
Building slowly up to heaven,
  Till our lives the lives shall seem
  Of the Master Builder's dream.

DOUGLAS MALLOCH

OUR TEMPLE

When our Temple of earth has been finished
   And our tools have been all laid aside,
When the sound of the gavel is silenced,
   And on earth we no longer reside,
We shall rise at the Word of the Master,
   And remember the way that we grew,
As the Master of All Good Workmen
   Shall put us to work anew.

And the faithful there shall be happy,
   As they sit near the Golden East
When the gifted shall scorn not the dullard,
   But aid both the great and the least.
We shall have real Masons to teach us,
   Solomon, Hiram, and Paul.
Whose lives have been squared by their service,
   As they gave to us of their all.

We there will build a new Temple,
   Reflecting the will of our God,
Its portals be easy to enter,
   For love is its entering rod.
Then each brother shall work without ceasing
   For the God whose dealings are square,
He will build the Temple of greatness
   For the God who in all things is fair.

And only the Master shall praise us,
   And only the Master shall blame,
And each for the love that is in him,
   With never a thought of fame,
Shall build his part of the Temple,
   With a care for each detail,
That will raise a perfect structure,
   A work that will never fail.

CHARLES CLYDE HUNT

When you rise in the morning, say that you will make the day blessed to a fellow creature. It is easily done: a left-off garment to the man who needs it: a kind word to the sorrowful; an encouraging expression to the struggling—trifles in themselves as light as air—will do at least for twenty-four hours. And if you are young, depend upon it, it will tell when you are old; and if you are old, rest assured it will send you gently down the stream of time to eternity. By the most simple arithmetical sum, look into the result. If you send one person away happy through the day, there are 365 in the course of a year. And suppose you live forty years only. After you commence that course of medicine, you have made 14,600 persons happy, at all events for a time.

ANONYMOUS

TOIL

THE BEE TOILS

The Bee does toil, builds pyramids of honeyed comb,
Stores gathered sweets in cupboards of its well-stocked home,
Mindful of those dependent on its daily toil,
And of the day, when flowers droop and shrouds entomb the soil.

MAN TOILS

Man too does toil, for honest toil brings happiness,
And cheers the heart of him whom God would bless.
Tuned to creation's teeming law divine,
Man labours well,—serene, contented and benign.

GOD TOILS

E'en God does toil, rears mountains full of hidden gold,
And frames those heights with flowered plains of marigold,
He tunes the song of angel, man and chickadee,
And guides the course of star and rock and growing tree.

WALTER H. BONN

THE GAUGE

The gauge divides the lives of men
    Until their lifetimes' tales are o'er;
Receive the Gauge, Apprentice, then,
    Consider well its hallowed lore!

A time for toil, a time for sleep,
    A time to serve such men as need,
The Craftsman thus his faith shall keep,
    As on the restless seasons speed.

For Work, whereby the peoples live,
    Much needs command its portion fair,
And labour shall the Craftsman give
    One-third his days, one-third his care.

And, weary when his tasks are done,
    The Craftsman lays him down to rest,
That he may greet the morrow's sun
    With fresher, slumber strengthened zest.

And work and rest himself shall raise
    Unto a higher, richer state,
To turn anew toward God, His praise,
    And succour the unfortunate.

A life well-lived is fashioned here,
    A life with joy and profit fraught:
Its round, through each success year,
    Is by this simple emblem taught.

R. J. McLAUCHLIN

THE TROWEL

The Perfect Ashlars, duly set
Within the walls, need mortar yet—
A Cement mixed with ancient skill,
And tempered at the Builder's will;
With this each crevice is concealed—
Each flaw and crack securely sealed,—
And all the blocks within their place
United in one perfect mass!

For this the Trowel's use is given,—
It makes the work secure and even;
Secure, that storms may not displace,
Even, that beauty's lines may grace;
It is the proof of Mason's art
Rightly to do the Trowel's part!
The rest is all reduced to rule,
But this must come from God's own school!

We build the "House not made with hands";
Our Master, from Celestial lands,
Points out the plan, the blocks, the place,
And bids us build in strength and grace:
From quarries' store we choose the rock,
We shape and smooth the perfect block,
And placing it upon the wall,
Humbly the Master's blessing call.

But there is yet a work undone,—
To fix the true and polished stone!
The Master's blessings will not fall
Upon a loose, disjointed wall;
Exposed to ravages of time,
It cannot have the mark sublime
That age and honour did bestow
Upon the FANE on Sion's brow.

Brothers, true Builders of the soul,
Would you become one perfect whole,
That all the blasts which time can move
Shall only strengthen you in love?
Would you, as Life's swift sands shall run,
Build up the Temple here begun,
That death's worst onset it may brave,
And you eternal wages have?

Then fix in love's cement the heart!
Study and act the Trowel's part!
Strive, in the Compass' span to live,
And mutual concessions give!
Daily your prayers and alms bestow,
As yonder light doth clearly show,
And walking by the Plummet just,
In God your hope, in God your trust!

ROBERT MORRIS

The artisan may give a man compass and square, but he cannot make
him skilful in the use of them.

As square and compass perfect squares and circles line,
Model of Human kinship's best, the Saint doth shine.

MENCIUS

Could we Heaven's will possess
As craftsman does his square
And the wheelwright his compass
Square and circles we could press.

MOTZU

68

The rung of a ladder was never meant to rest upon, but only to hold a man's foot long enough to enable him to put his other foot somewhat higher.

THOMAS HUXLEY

THE ROAD OF MASONRY

Men build a road of Masonry
    Across the hills and dales,
Unite the prairie and the sea,
    The mountains and the vales.
They cross the chasm, bridge the stream,
They point to where the turrets gleam,
    And many men for many a day
    Who seek the heights shall find the way.

Men build a road of Masonry,
    But not for self they build:
With footsteps of humanity
    The hearts of men are thrilled.
This music makes their labour sweet:
The endless tramp of other feet,
    The thought that men shall travel thus
    An easier road because of us.

We build the road of Masonry
    With other men in mind;
We do not build for you and me,
    We build for all mankind.
We build a road!—remember, men,
Build not for Now, but build for Then,
    And other men who walk the way
    Shall find the road we built today.

Who builds the road of Masonry,
    Though small or great his part,
However hard the task may be,
    May toil with singing heart.
For it is something, after all,
When muscles tire and shadows fall,
    To know that other men shall bless
    The builder for his faithfulness.

DOUGLAS MALLOCH

ENAMOURED ARCHITECT OF AIRY RHYME

Enamoured architect of airy rhyme,
Build as thou wilt; heed not what each man says:
Good souls, but innocent of dreamers' ways,
Will come, and marvel why thou wastest time;
Others, beholding how thy turrets climb
'Twixt theirs and heaven, will hate thee all thy days;
But most beware of those who come to praise.
O Wondersmith, O worker in sublime
And heaven-sent dreams, let art be all in all;
Build as thou wilt, unspoiled by praise or blame,
Build as thou wilt, and as thy light is given:
Then, if at last the airy structure fall,
Dissolve, and vanish—take thyself no shame.
They fail, and they alone, who have not striven.

THOMAS BAILEY ALDRICH

That thing which I understand by real art is the expression by man of his pleasure in labour. I do not believe he can be happy in his labour without expressing that happiness; and especially is this so when he is at work at anything in which he specially excels. A most kind gift is this of nature, since all men, nay, it seems all things, too, must labour; so that not only does the dog take pleasure in hunting and the horse in running, and the bird in flying, but so natural does the idea seem to us, that we imagine to ourselves that the earth and the very elements rejoice in doing their appointed work; and the poets have told us of the spring meadows smiling, of the exultations of the fire, of the countless laughter of the sea.

WILLIAM MORRIS

MY ASHLAR

O, Master Builder, here I bring
This ashlar as my offering—
This block entrusted to my care—
O, try it by Thy faultless square.
Prove Thou the stone which I have brought,
Judge Thou the task my hands have wrought—
My hands unskilled! Ah, much I fear
Their work imperfect shall appear.

See, Master, here were corners rough
Which marred the stone, so stubborn, tough,
They long withstood my gavel's blow;
What toil they cost, Thou mayest know.
My zeal I own did often swoon
Ere from the ashlar they were hewn;
(Ah, vice and habit, conquered now,
With agony you wrung my brow.)

Crushed by the load of guilt I bear,
O, Master, look on my despair,
For where was drawn Thy fair design
My plan appears in many a line.
Hot tears, alas, cannot efface
The flaws which speak of my disgrace;
Too late the mischief to undo,
My ashlar I submit to you.

71

O, Master, grant this boon to me;
Unworthy though my stone may be,
Cast it not utterly away,
But let it rest beside the way
Where its grave flaws may warning be
To him who follows after me.
If he thereby my faults may shun,
I'll feel some grain of worth I've won.

GEORGE H. FREE

THE GAVEL

Within the quarry, I, the youngest Craftsman, stood,
And there were, all about me, mighty blocks
Rough-hewn from out the granite breast of Earth:

So young was I, so foolish and so fond,
That, as I stood, I mused upon myself,
Beholding in my person perfect things,
And, as I meditated there, I spoke:
Said I, "Observe in me the ages' heir,
Complete Fulfilment's type and Wisdom's son;
Let Future view my parts and there remark
Its sound salvation, its embodied hope,
For, as I stand, I am the very plinth,
Square-set, whereon its beauty may be built."

A cloud slid down, the moon's fair face was hid,
And, with the darkness, came a curious thing;
A voice, profound, reproving, kind withal,
Proceeded from the centre of the stone
And, fearful, I attended as it spoke;
The living boulder, grown articulate.

"Fond Youth," it told me, "we, thy comrades, speak
Such words as thine when first our shapes assume
Some likeness to the polished ashlars which

72

Compose the Temple's fair and perfect strength:
But ere our mass may be of any use
Lo, are we changed till none that sees us now
Might know us then; and only that remains
Which age's processes have given us;
Stones are we still, as ye are always men,
But stones prepared by toil and pain and sweat;
And thou, my foolish one, art like to us,
A mighty hulk of vast potential strength,
Potential wisdom, beauty, too, no doubt,
But none of these as yet nor will be till
Though are prepared, like us, by toil and sweat;
Consider thou the Gavel, let it break
Thee to some fitting semblance of a man,
Else be thou silent, patient to remain
Within the quarry, with thy brother stones."
The cloud slid up, soft light caressed the scene
And all about were simple, mighty blocks
Rough-hewn from out the granite breast of Earth,
Great, futile, massy, purposeless and dumb,
And I was one of them.

R. J. MCLAUCHLIN

KING SOLOMON'S TEMPLE

There's a Temple of God in tales of the past,
   I see through the mists of historical years.
And my heart through the veil of its mysteries vast
   Is filled with the vision of numberless spheres,
Revealing my failure to build temples to last
   Through the age after age that before me appears.

With the stars of my God ever shining above,
   And the tools of my calling at hand,
I will build me a temple of glorious love,
   With the arch of my Masonry spanned.
And the Spirit of God coming down from above
   Will comfort my soul with His wand.

There's a Mountain of God in each of our hearts
  For that temple's enduring base.
And the work we may do by a Mason's arts
  Will this solid foundation embrace.
And within it's a spirit that never departs
  Nor will ever the temple disgrace.

Through the beautiful aisles of the glorious past
  Will its wonderful harmonies swell,
When the dead shall arise at Gabriel's blast
  From the grave's most darkening cell.
Then the lot of the true will no longer be cast
  With the false he ought to repel.

"The Cedars of Lebanon grow at our door,
  The quarries are found at our gate,
The ships out of Ophir with golden ore,
  For our summoning mandate wait."
Then let us get busy (day soon'll be o'er)
  And the house of our soul we'll create.

While the light is still with us, the light should be used
  For the night we cannot control.
Or ever the silver cord be loosed,
  Or be broken the golden bowl.
May we build the Temple we never can lose
  For the dwelling place of our soul.

CHARLES CLYDE HUNT

Hate never builds anything; it can only blast,
Every beautiful thing has been loved into being.

JOSEPH FORT NEWTON

74

THE VOICE OF AMERICA

I have taken the breed of all nations,
   Barred no religion or race;
From the highest and lowest of stations
   They came—and I found them place.

Powers invisible drew them,
   Freedom unborn was their quest,
'Til my uttermost borderlands knew them—
   The least of the world and the best.

They came with the wisdom of sages,
   The darkness, the stain and the dirt,
They came with the glory of ages,
   And I took them—my hope and my hurt.

I have gathered the breed of all nations,
   Drawn from each caste and each clan;
Tried them and proved them and loved them
   And made them American.

Made them a nation of Builders,
   Fearless and faithful and free,
Entered them, passed them and raised them
   To the Master's Sublime Degree.

Theirs is the task of restoring
   The Ancient and Honoured Guild—
The work to the Speculative,
   The spirit to those who build.

'Til none shall be less than a Master,
   And know but one Ruler above,
Bound by the spirit of justice
   And the mortar of brotherly love.

'Til the house shall belong to the Workman
   And the Craft come again to its own;
And this is your task, oh, my people!
   Through you will the Lost Word be known.

JOSEPHINE B. BOWMAN

Higher Thoughts— Greater Achievements

THE HIDDEN MEANING

A Mason's ways are
   A type of existence,
   And his persistence
Is as the days are
   Of men in the world.

The future hides in it
   Good hap or sorrow,
   We pass through it—
Naught there abides in it
   Daunting us—onward.

And silent, before us,
   Veiled the dark portal,
   Goal of all mortal:
Stars silent rest over us,
   Graves under us silent.

But heard are the voices—
   Voices of the sages
   Of the world and the ages—
Choose well, your choice is
   Brief, but yet endless.

Here eyes do regard you
   In eternity's stillness,
   Here is all fullness,
Ye brave, to reward you,
   Work, and despair not.

JOHANN WOLFGANG VON GOETHE

THE APRON

Guard thou this Apron even as thy soul!
High Badge it is of an undaunted band,
Which, from the dawn of dim forgotten time,
Has struggled upward in a quest of light—
Light that is found in reverence of self,
Unselfish Brother-love and love of God.

This light now on thine Apron shines undimmed;
Let ne'er a shadow intercept its beams.
Thine eyes late saw the Sun burst from the East
Marking the Morn of thy Masonic day,
Calling thee forth to labour with thy peers,
Gird then thy lambskin on; nor fail to find
In it a thought of brooks and sweet clean fields,
Haunts of this lamb through many a sunny hour.
Find in it, too, a nobler thought of Him
The Light ineffable, that Lamb of God,
Immaculate, unstained by shame or sin,
Who dying left ensample to all men
Who would build lives in purity and truth.

In Wisdom plan thy Apprentice task; divide
Thy time with care, thy moments spend as though
Each day were lifelong, life but as a day.
In purity of heart and sheer integrity
Use thou the gavel on each stubborn edge,
Divesting thought of aught perchance might stain,
Or scar, or tear this badge of shining white.

At midday in the Craft's high fellowship,
Gird round thy life these bands of loyal blue,
Uniting with thee all to thee akin.
Strong in a deepening knowledge, bend thy skill
To levelling false pride in place attained,
To squaring thy foundations with the truth,
To setting each new stone in rectitude.

When in the West the Evening turns to gold
And beautifies what Strength and Wisdom reared,
Pause not, but search thy trestle-board, God's plan;

And ply with solemn joy thy master tools,
Earth's many cementing into heaven's one.
Full soon an unseen Hand shall gently stay
Thine arm; and on thine Apron, scutcheon bright,
Shall rest the All-seeing Eye, adjudging there
The blazoned record of thy workmanship.
Anon, thy Sun goes out and brothers lay,
With thee, thine Apron in the breast of earth,
Among the forgetful archives of the dust.

Wear worthily this thy Masonic badge,
While still thy body toils to build thy soul
A mansion bright, beyond the gates of death,
No edifice that crumbles back to clay,
But a glorious house eternal in the skies.

These, now, be Mason's wages; when from his hands
Forever fall the working tools of life,
Arising, to ascend to loftier work;—
From out the lowly quarries to be called
To labour in the City of the King;—
Glad in the light of one long endless day,
To serve anew the Celestial Architect
And Sovereign Master of the Lodge Above.

Thy portion, Brother, may it be to hear
These welcome words, when the great Judge shall scan
Thy work, "Well done! Thou good and faithful servant,
Enter thou into the joy of thy Lord."

J. HUBERT SCOTT

RULES FOR THE ROAD

Stand straight;
Step firmly, throw your weight:
The heaven is high above your head
And the good grey road is faithful to your tread.

Be strong:
Sing to your heart a battle song:
Though hidden foemen lie in wait,
Something is in you that can smile at Fate.

Press through:
Nothing can harm if you are true.
And when the night comes, rest:
The earth is friendly as a mother's breast.

EDWIN MARKHAM

Sad is the day for any man when he becomes absolutely satisfied with
the life he is living, the thoughts that he is thinking and the deeds that
he is doing; when there ceases to be forever beating at the doors of
his soul a desire to do something larger which he feels and knows he
was meant and intended to do.

PHILLIPS BROOKS

ON PRESENTING THE LAMBSKIN APRON

Light and white are its leathern folds;
And a priceless lesson its texture holds.
Symbol it is, as the years increase,
Of the paths that lead through the fields of Peace.
Type it is of the higher sphere,
Where the deeds of the body, ended here,
Shall one by one the by-way be
To pass the gates of Eternity.

Emblem it is of a life intense,
Held aloof from the world of sense;
Of the upright walk and the lofty mind,
Far from the dross of Earth inclined.
Sign it is that he who wears
Its sweep unsullied, about him bears
That which should be to mind and heart,
A set reminder of his art.

So may it ever bring to thee
The high resolves of Purity.
Its spotless field of shining white,
Serve to guide thy steps aright;
Thy daily life, in scope and plans,
Be that of the strong and upright man.
And signal shall the honour be
Unto those who wear it worthily.

Receive it thus to symbolize
Its drift, in the life that before thee lies.
Badge as it is of a great degree,
Be it chart and compass unto thee.

FAY HEMPSTEAD

THE WHITE LEATHER APRON

The white leather apron is more ancient by far
Than the eagles of Rome, a symbol of war,
Or the fleece of pure gold, by emperors given,
A rich decoration for which many have striven.
The Garter of England, an Order most rare,
Although highly prized, can not with it compare;
It is an emblem of innocence, symbolled in white,
And purity ever brings the greatest delight;
With pure thoughts and actions, how happy the life,
How care-free the conscience, unclouded by strife!

No Potentate ever can upon us bestow
An honour so great as this apron doth show;
No king on his throne in his highest estate
Can give us an emblem so cherished or great;
'Tis the Badge of a Mason, more noble to wear
Than the gold of the mine, or the diamond most rare.
So here's to the lambskin, the apron of white,
That lifts up all equals and all doth unite,
In the Order so ancient that man can not say
When its teachings began or name its birthday.

Since its birth, nations young have gone to their tomb,
And cities once great turned to ashes and gloom;
Earth's greatest achievements have long passed away,
And peoples have risen and gone to decay.
Outliving all these, never changing with time,
Are the principles taught in our Order sublime.
And now, my good brother, this apron's for you,
May you worthily wear it and ever be true
To the vows you have made, to the lessons most grand;
For these, home and country, we ever will stand.

D. W. CLEMENTS

BE THE BEST OF WHATEVER YOU ARE

If you can't be a pine on the top of the hill,
  Be a scrub in the valley—but be
The best little scrub by the side of the rill;
  Be a bush if you can't be a tree.

If you can't be a bush be a bit of the grass,
  And some highway happier make;
If you can't be a muskie then just be a bass—
  But the liveliest bass in the lake!

We can't all be captains, we've got to be crew,
  There's something for all of us here,
There's big work to do, and there's lesser to do,
  And the task you must do is the near.

If you can't be a highway then just be a trail,
  If you can't be the sun be a star;
It isn't by size that you win or you fail—
  Be the best of whatever you are!

DOUGLAS MALLOCH

PERSEVERANCE

If a task is once begun
Never leave it till it's done.
Be the labour great or small,
Do it well or not at all.

ANONYMOUS

PRESS ON

Press on! Surmount the rocky steps,
    Climb boldly o'er the torrent's arch;
He fails alone who feebly creeps,
    He wins who dares the hero's march.
Be thou a hero! Let thy might
    Tramp on eternal snows its way,
And through the ebon walls of night
    Hew down a passage unto day.

Press on! If once and twice thy feet
    Slip back and stumble, harder try;
From him who never dreads to meet
    Danger and death they're sure to fly.
To coward ranks the bullet speeds,
    While on their breasts who never quail,
Gleams, guardian of chivalric deeds,
    Bright courage like a coat of mail.

Press on! If Fortune play thee false
    To-day, to-morrow she'll be true;
Whom now she sinks she now exalts,
    Taking old gifts and granting new,
The wisdom of the present hour
    Makes up the follies past and gone;
To weakness strength succeeds, and power
    From frailty springs! Press on, press on!

PARK BENJAMIN

TO-DAY

Sure, this world is full of trouble—
    I ain't said it ain't.
Lord! I've had enough, an' double,
    Reason for complaint.
Rain an' storm have come to fret me,
    Skies were often grey;
Thorns an' brambles have beset me
    On the road—but, say,
    Ain't it fine to-day?

What's the use of always weepin',
    Makin' trouble last?
What's the use of always keepin'
    Thinkin' of the past?
Each must have his tribulation,
    Water with his wine.
Life it ain't no celebration.
    Trouble? I've had mine—
    But to-day is fine.

It's to-day that I am livin',
    Not a month ago,
Havin', losin', takin', givin',
    As time wills it so.
Yesterday a cloud of sorrow
    Fell across the way;
It may rain again to-morrow,
    It may rain—but, say,
    Ain't it fine to-day!

                DOUGLAS MALLOCH

ONE WHO NEVER TURNED HIS BACK

One who never turned his back but marched breast forward;
    Never doubted clouds would break;
Never dreamed, though right were worsted, wrong would
    triumph;
    Held we fall to rise, are baffled to fight better,
        Sleep to wake.

No, at noonday in the bustle of man's work-time
Greet the unseen with a cheer!
Bid him forward, breast and back as either should be,
"Strive and thrive!" cry "Speed,—fight on, fare ever
There as here!"

ROBERT BROWNING

QUIT YOU LIKE MEN

Quit you like men, be strong;
  There's a burden to bear,
  There's a grief to share,
  There's a heart that breaks 'neath a load of care—
But fare ye forth with a song.

Quit you like men, be strong;
  There's a battle to fight,
  There's a wrong to right,
  There's a God who blesses the good with might—
So fare ye forth with a song.

Quit you like men, be strong;
  There's a work to do,
  There's a world to make new,
  There's a call for men who are brave and true—
On! on with the song!

Quit you like men, be strong;
  There's a year of grace,
  There's a God to face,
  There's another heat in the great world race—
Speed, speed with a song!

WILLIAM HERBERT HUDNUT

THE MASTER'S APRON

Ther's mony a badge that's unco braw;
   Wi' ribbon, lace and tape on;
Let kings an' princes wear them a'
   Gie me the Master's apron!

The honest craftsman's apron,
The jolly Freemason's apron,
Be he at hame, or roam afar,
Before his touch fa's bolt and bar,
The gates of fortune fly ajar,
'Gin he but wears the apron!

For wealth and honour, pride and power
   Are crumbling stanes to base on;
Fraternity suld rule the hour,
   And ilka worthy Mason!
   Each Free Accepted Mason,
   Each Ancient Crafted Mason.

Then, brithers, let a halesome sang
Arise your friendly ranks alang!
Guidwives and bairnies blithely sing
To the ancient badge wi' the apron string
That is worn by the Master Mason!

ROBERT BURNS

We are not weak if we make a proper use of those means which the
God of Nature has placed in our power . . . the battle, sir, is not to
the strong alone; it is to the vigilant, the active, the brave.

PATRICK HENRY

TRY, TRY AGAIN

'Tis a lesson you should heed,
   Try, try again;
If at first you don't succeed,
   Try, try again;
Then your courage should appear,
For, if you will persevere,
You will conquer, never fear;
   Try, try again.

Once or twice though you should fail,
   Try, try again;
If you would at last prevail,
   Try, try again;
If we strive, 'tis no disgrace
Though we do not win the race;
What should you do in the case?
   Try, try again.

Time will bring you your reward,
   Try, try again.
All that other folks can do,
Why, with patience, should not you?
Only keep this rule in view:
   Try, try again.

ANONYMOUS

TRY THE SQUARE

Is a Brother off the track?
   Try the Square;
  Try it well on every side.
Nothing draws a craftsman back
  Like the Square when well applied.
   Try the Square.

Is he crooked, is he frail?
    Try the Square.
  Try it early, try it late;
When all other efforts fail,
    Try the Square to make him straight—
    Try the Square.

Does he still persist in wrong?
    Try the Square.
  Loves he darkness more than light?
Try it thorough, try it long.
    Try the Square to make him right—
    Try the Square.

Fails the Square to bring him in?
    Try the Square.
  Be not sparing of the pains;
While there's any work to do,
    While a crook or knot remains—
    Try the Square.

DAVID BARKER

Continue to make the demands of the day your immediate concern, and take occasion to test the purity of your hearts and the steadfastness of your spirits. When you then take a deep breath and rise above the cares of this world in an hour of leisure, you will surely win the proper frame of mind to face devoutly what is above us, with reverence, seeing in all events the manifestation of a higher guidance.

JOHANN WOLFGANG VON GOETHE

THE WHITE LEATHER APRON

Here's a toast to the Lambskin, more ancient by far
Than the fleece of pure gold or the eagles of war;
'Tis an emblem of innocence, nobler to wear
Than the Garter of England or order as rare.

Let the king wear the purple and point to his crown
Which may fall from his brow when his throne tumbles down;
But the badge of a Mason has much more to give
Than a kingdom so frail that it cannot long live.

Let the field-marshal boast of the men he can guide,
Of the infantry columns and the heroes that ride;
But the White Leather Apron his standard outranks,
Since it waves from the East to the Death River's banks.

'Tis the shield of the orphan, the hostage of love;
'Tis the charter of Faith in the Grand Lodge above;
While the high and the low, in its whiteness arrayed,
Of one blood and one kin by its magic are made.

Kingdoms fall to the earth; cities crumble to dust;
Men are born but to die; swords are made but to rust;
But the White Leather Apron, through ages passed on,
Has survived with the lodge of the Holy St. John.

So a toast to the Lambskin, which levels, uplifts—
To the White Leather Apron, most priceless of gifts.
'Tis the badge of a Mason, more ancient by far
Than the fleece of pure gold or the eagles of war.

FRANKLYN W. LEE

TODAY

So here hath been dawning
    Another blue day:
Think, wilt thou let it
    Slip useless away?

Out of Eternity
    This new day was born;
Into Eternity,
    At night, will return.

Behold it aforetime
No eye ever did;
So soon it forever
From all eyes is hid.

Here hath been dawning
Another blue day:
Think, wilt thou let it
Slip useless away?

THOMAS CARLYLE

There are but two ways which lead to great aims and achievements—
energy and perseverance. Energy is a rare gift,—it provokes opposition, hatred, and reaction. But perseverance lies within the affordings
of everyone, its power increases with its progress, and it but rarely
misses its aim.

JOHANN WOLFGANG VON GOETHE

BRAVE LIFE

I do not know what I shall find on out beyond the final fight;
I do not know what I shall meet beyond the last barrage of night;
Nor do I care—but this I know—if I but serve within the fold
And play the game—I'll be prepared for all the endless years may hold.

Life is a training camp at best for what may wait beyond the years;
A training camp of toiling days and nights that lean to dreams and
tears;
But each may come upon the goal, and build his soul above all Fate
By holding an unbroken faith and taking Courage for a mate.

89

Is not the fight itself enough that man must look to some behest?
Wherein does Failure miss Success if all engaged but do their best?
Where does the Victor's cry come in for wreath of fame or laurelled
    brow
If one he vanquished fought as well as weaker muscle would allow?

If my opponent in the fray should prove to be a stronger foe—
Not of his making—but because the Destinies ordained if so;
If he should win—and I should lose—although I did my utmost part,
Is my reward the less than his if he should strive with equal heart?

Brave Life, I hold, is something more than driving upward to the peak;
Than smashing madly through the strong, and crashing onward
    through the weak;
I hold the man who makes his fight against the raw game's crushing
    odds
Is braver than his brothers are who hold the favour of the gods.

On by the sky line, faint and vague, in that Far Country all must know,
No laurel crown of fame may wait beyond the sunset's glow;
But life has given me the chance to train and serve within the fold,
To meet the test—and be prepared for all the endless years may hold.

GRANTLAND RICE

LORD, MAKE A REGULAR MAN OUT OF ME

This I would like to be—braver and bolder,
Just a bit wiser because I am older,
Just a bit kinder to those I may meet,
Just a bit manlier taking defeat;
This for the New Year my wish and my plea—
Lord, make a regular man out of me.

This I would like to be—just a bit finer,
More of a smiler and less of a whiner,
Just a bit quicker to stretch out my hand
Helping another who's struggling to stand,
This is my prayer for the New Year to be,
Lord, make a regular man out of me.

This I would like to be—just a bit fairer,
Just a bit better, and just a bit squarer,
Not quite so ready to censure and blame,
Quicker to help every man in the game,
Not quite so eager men's failings to see,
Lord, make a regular man out of me.

This I would like to be—just a bit truer,
Less of the wisher and more of the doer,
Broader and bigger, more willing to give,
Living and helping my neighbour to live!
This for the New Year my prayer and my plea—
Lord, make a regular man out of me.

EDGAR A. GUEST

MYSELF

I have to live with myself, and so
I want to be fit for myself to know,
I want to be able, as days go by,
Always to look myself straight in the eye;
I don't want to stand, with the setting sun,
And hate myself for things I have done.

I don't want to keep on a closet shelf
A lot of secrets about myself,
And fool myself, as I come and go,
Into thinking that nobody else will know
The kind of a man I really am;
I don't want to dress up myself in sham.

I want to go out with my head erect,
I want to deserve all men's respect;
But here in the struggle for fame and pelf
I want to be able to like myself.
I don't want to look at myself and know
That I'm bluster and bluff and empty show.

I can never hide myself from me;
I see what others may never see;
I know what others may never know,
I never can fool myself, and so,
Whatever happens, I want to be
Self-respecting and conscience free.

EDGAR A. GUEST

Do not pray for easy lives; pray to be stronger men. Do not pray for
tasks equal to your powers; pray for power equal to your tasks.

PHILLIPS BROOKS

THE NOBLENESS OF WORK

There is a perennial nobleness, and even sacredness, in Work. Were
he never so benighted, forgetful of his high calling, there is always
hope in a man that actually and earnestly works; in Idleness alone is
there perpetual despair. . . .

THOMAS CARLYLE

DUTY

When Duty comes a-knocking at your gate,
Welcome him in, for if you bid him wait,
He will depart only to come once more
And bring seven other duties to your door.

EDWIN MARKHAM

MINE—

(Rondeau, after Dobson)

My Cable-tow, a tie most blessed!
In Master's East and Warden's West
And Mason's faith, a corner-stone
For Craftsmen all; for each alone
The ancient bond of all oppressed.

Its wisdom, deep within the breast,
Grows more as less it is confessed,
  This silver cord through ages grown,
  My Cable-tow.

A mystery; much less a test
Than riddle, dearer that unguessed.
  What I know not I've always known;
  My brother's tie is most my own
Dear symbol of a ceaseless quest,
  My Cable-tow.

CARL H. CLAUDY

I do the very best I know how—the very best I can; and I mean to keep doing so until the end. If the end brings me out all right, what is said against me won't amount to anything. If the end brings me out wrong, ten angels swearing I was right would make no difference.

ABRAHAM LINCOLN

OPPORTUNITY

In an old city by the storied shores
Where the bright summit of Olympus soars,
A cryptic statue mounted towards the light—
Heel-winged, tip-toed, and poised for instant flight.

"O statue, tell your name," a traveller cried,
And solemnly the marble lips replied:
"Men call me Opportunity: I lift
My winged feet from earth to show how swift
My flight, how short my stay—
How Fate is ever waiting on the way."

"But why that tossing ringlet on your brow?"
"That men may seize me any moment: *Now*,
NOW is my other name: to-day my date:
O traveller, to-morrow is too late!"

EDWIN MARKHAM

One hour of life, crowded to the full with glorious action, and filled
with noble risks, is worth whole years of those mean observances of
paltry decorum, in which men steal through existence, like sluggish
waters through a marsh, without either honour or observation.

SIR WALTER SCOTT

Think wrongly, if you please, but in all cases think for yourself.

GOTTHOLD EPHRAIM LESSING

BANQUET NIGHT

"Once in so often," King Solomon said,
    Watching his quarrymen drill the stone,
"We will club our garlic and wine and bread
    And banquet together beneath my Throne.
And all the Brethren shall come to that mess
As Fellow-Craftsmen—no more and no less.

"Send a swift shallop to Hiram of Tyre,
    Felling and floating our beautiful trees,
Say that the Brethren and I desire
    Talk with our Brethren who use the seas.
And we shall be happy to meet them at mess
As Fellow-Craftsmen—no more and no less.

"Carry this message to Hiram Abif—
    Excellent Master of forge and mine:—
I and the Brethren would like it if
    He and the Brethren will come to dine
(Garments from Bozrah or morning-dress)
As Fellow-Craftsmen—no more and no less.

"God gave the Hyssop and Cedar their place—
    Also the Bramble, the Fig and the Thorn—
But that is no reason to black a man's face
    Because he is not what he hasn't been born.
And, as touching the Temple, I hold and profess
We are Fellow-Craftsmen—no more and no less."

So it was ordered and so it was done,
    And the hewers of wood and the Masons of Mark,
With foc'sle hands of the Sidon run
    And Navy Lords from the ROYAL ARK,
Came and sat down and were merry at mess
As Fellow-Craftsmen—no more and no less.

The Quarries are hotter than Hiram's forge,
    No one is safe from the dog-whips' reach.
It's mostly snowing up Lebanon gorge,
    And it's always blowing off Joppa beach;
But once in so often, the messenger brings
Solomon's mandate: "Forget these things!
Brother to Beggars and Fellow to Kings,
Companion of Princes—forget these things!
Fellow-Craftsman, forget these things!"

RUDYARD KIPLING

95

WHEN NATURE WANTS A MAN

When Nature wants to drill a man
And thrill a man,
And skill a man,
When Nature wants to mould a man
To play the noblest part;
When she yearns with all her heart
To create so great and bold a man
That all the world shall praise—
Watch her method, watch her ways!
How she ruthlessly perfects
Whom she royally elects;
How she hammers him and hurts him
And with mighty blows converts him
Into trial shapes of clay which only Nature understands—
While his tortured heart is crying and he lifts beseeching
    hands!—
How she bends, but never breaks,
When his good she undertakes . . .
How she uses whom she chooses
And with every purpose fuses him,
By every art induces him
To try his splendour out—
Nature knows what she's about.

When Nature wants to take a man
And shake a man
And wake a man;
When Nature wants to make a man
To do the Future's will;
When she tries with all her skill
And she yearns with all her soul
To create him large and whole . . .
With what cunning she prepares him!
How she goads and never spares him,
How she whets him and she frets him
And in poverty begets him . . .
How she often disappoints
Whom she sacredly anoints,

With what wisdom she will hide him,
Never minding what betide him
Though his genius sob with slighting and his pride may not
     forget!
Bids him struggle harder yet.
Makes him lonely
So that only
God's high messages shall reach him
So that she may surely teach him
What the Hierarchy planned.
Though he may not understand
Gives him passions to command—
How remorselessly she spurs him,
With terrific ardour stirs him
When she poignantly prefers him!

When Nature wants to name a man
And fame a man
And tame a man;
When Nature wants to shame a man
To do his heavenly best . . .
When she tries the highest test
That her reckoning may bring—
When she wants a god or king!—
How she reins him and restrains him
So his body scarce contains him
While she fires him
And inspires him!
Keeps him yearning, ever burning for a tantalising goal—
Lures and lacerates his soul.
Sets a challenge for his spirit,
Draws it higher when he's near it—
Makes a jungle, that he clear it;
Makes a desert, that he fear it
And subdue it if he can—
So doth Nature make a man.
Then, to test his spirit's wrath
Hurls a mountain in his path—
Puts a bitter choice before him
And relentless stands o'er him.
"Climb, or perish!" so she says . . .
Watch her purpose, watch her ways!

Nature's plan is wondrous kind
Could we understand her mind . . .
Fools are they who call her blind.
When his feet are torn and bleeding
Yet his spirit mounts unheeding,
All his higher powers speeding
Blazing newer paths and fine;
When the force that is divine
Leaps to challenge every failure and his ardour still is sweet
And love and hope are burning in the presence of defeat . . .
Lo, the crisis! Lo, the shout
That must call the leader out.
When the people need salvation
    Doth he come to lead the nation . . .
Then doth Nature show her plan
When the world has found—a man!

ANGELA MORGAN

THE ABSENT ONE

Tonight I sat before an altar high
Brighter than any work of human hands.
From faintly glinting censers, swinging low,
Thin spiral threads of smoke ascending slow
Faded into the faulted darkness overhead.
From some unseen choir, far away, there came
Thin voices bearing melodies not of earth.
From these, the sanctuary, the lights, the music faint,
There came a peace as though some fair hand
With tender touch had smoothed my aching brow,
And wiped away the cumbering cares of day.
The miracle was thine; through many miles
Thy thought, thy love had reached and brought
To me warm consolation to a hungry heart.

ERNEST R. MOORE

WHO HAS KNOWN HEIGHTS

Who has known heights and depths shall not again
   Know peace—not as the calm heart knows
   Low, ivied walls; a garden close;
   The old enchantment of a rose.
And though he tread the humble ways of men
He shall not speak the common tongue again.

Who has known heights shall bear forevermore
   An incommunicable thing
   That hurts his heart, as if a wing
   Beat at the portal, challenging;
And yet—lured by the gleam his vision wore—
Who once has trodden stars seeks peace no more.

                MARY BRENT WHITESIDE

ATTAINMENT

With every rising of the sun,
Think of your life as just begun,
The past has cancelled and buried deep
All yesterdays: there let them sleep.
Concern yourself with but today;
Grasp it and teach it to obey
Your will and plan.
Since time began, today has been
The friend of man.
You and today: a soul sublime
And the great heritage of time.
With God himself to bid the twain,
"Go forth, brave heart; attain! Attain!"

                ANONYMOUS

THE HEIGHTS

The heights by great men reached and kept
Were not attained by sudden flight,
But they, while their companions slept
Were toiling upward in the night.

HENRY WADSWORTH LONGFELLOW

He has achieved success who has lived well, laughed often, and loved much, who has gained the respect of intelligent men and the love of little children; who has filled his niche and accomplished his task; who has left the world better than he found it, whether by an improved poppy, a perfect poem, or a rescued soul; who has never lacked appreciation of earth's beauty or failed to express it; who has always looked for the best in others and given the best he had; whose life was an inspiration, whose memory a benediction.

ANONYMOUS

Wisdom, Strength, and Beauty

When is a man a Mason? When he can look out over the rivers, the hills, and the far horizon with a profound sense of his own littleness in the vast scheme of things, and yet have faith, hope, and courage. When he knows that down in his heart every man is as noble, as vile, as divine, as diabolic, and as lonely as himself, and seeks to know, to forgive, and to love his fellow man. When he knows how to sympathize with men in their sorrows, yea, even in their sins—knowing that each man fights a hard fight against many odds. When he has learned how to make friends and to keep them, and above all how to keep friends with himself. When he loves flowers, can hunt the birds without a gun, and feels the thrill of an old forgotten joy when he hears the laugh of a little child. When he can be happy and high-minded amid the meaner drudgeries of life. When star-crowned trees and the glint of sunlight on flowing waters subdue him like the thought of one much loved and long dead. When no voice of distress reaches his ears in vain, and no hand seeks his aid without response. When he finds good in every faith that helps any man to lay hold of higher things, and to see majestic meanings in life, whatever the name of that faith may be. When he can look into a wayside puddle and see something besides mud, and into the face of the most forlorn mortal and see something beyond sin. When he knows how to pray, how to love, how to hope. When he has kept faith with himself, with his fellow man, with his God; in his hand a sword for evil, in his heart a bit of a song—glad to live, but not afraid to die! In such a man, whether he be rich or poor, scholarly or unlearned, famous or obscure, Masonry has wrought her sweet ministry! Such a man has found the only real secret of Masonry, and the one which it is trying to give to all the world.

JOSEPH FORT NEWTON

Pure wisdom always directs itself toward God; the purest wisdom is knowledge of God.

LEW WALLACE

A MASON'S GREETING

To all who hope for life beyond this living,
  To all who reverence one holy Name—
Whose liberal hand will not be stayed from giving,
  Who count all human fellowship the same;
Whose lives ascend in wisdom, strength, and beauty,
  Stone upon stone, square-hewn and founded well,
Who love the light—who tread the path of duty:
  Greet you well, brethren! Brethren, greet you well!

JOHN EDMUND BARSS

AN OLD MASONIC TOAST

"To him that all things understood,
  To him that found the stone and wood,
  To him that hapless lost his blood
    In doing of his duty.
  To that blest age, and that blest morn
  Wherein those three great men were born,
  Our noble science to adorn
    With Wisdom, Strength and Beauty."

ANONYMOUS

TO STRETCH THE LIBERAL HAND

To stretch the liberal hand,
  And pour the stream of gladness
O'er misery's withered strand,—
  To cheer the hearth of sadness,—
To dry the orphan's tear,
  And soothe the heart nigh broken,—
To breathe in sorrow's ear
  Kind words in kindness spoken,—
    This is the Mason's part,
      The Mason's bounden duty,
    This rears the Mason's heart
      In wisdom, strength and beauty.

To practice virtue's laws
   With fervency and freedom,
And in her noble cause
   Advance where'er she lead 'em,—
To curb the headlong course
   Of passion's fiery pinion,
And bend its stubborn force
   To reason's mild dominion,—
      This is the Mason's part,
         The Mason's bounden duty,
      This rears the Mason's heart
         In wisdom, strength and beauty.

To shield a brother's fame
   From envy and detraction,
And prove that truth's our aim
   In spirit, life and action,—
To trust in God, through all
   The danger and temptation,
Which to his lot may fall,
   In trial and probation,—
      This is the Mason's part,
         The Mason's bounden duty,
      This rears the Mason's heart
         In wisdom, strength and beauty.

ANONYMOUS

All that has reference to what is eternal, all that in our earthly life by
way of image or parable suggests what is imperishable, should rightly
not be made the subject of debate, difficult though such exclusion may
be. For, in so far as we translate our ways of thinking and feeling into
terms of outward circumstance, in so far as we form a society about
us or join such a one, something belonging to the inner world becomes
externalized. What is thus established, whether received with favour or
disfavour, must be maintained and defended. And so, despite ourselves,
we have made a retreat from the realm of the spiritual to that of the
secular, from the celestial to the earthly, and from the eternal and
immutable to what is subject to the laws of time and change.

JOHANN WOLFGANG VON GOETHE

THE WORKING TOOLS

Let us be *true*,—each Working Tool
  The Master places in our care
Imparts a stern but wholesome rule,
  To all who work and journey here;
    The Architect Divine has used
    The Plumb, the Level and the Square.

Let us be *wise; the Level*, see!
  How certain is the doom of man!
So humble should Freemasons be
  Who work within this narrow span;
    No room for pride and vanity—
    Let wisdom rule our every plan.

Let us be *just;* behold *the Square!*
  Its pattern deviates no part
From that which, in the Master's care,
  Tries all the angles of the heart.
    O sacred implement divine,—
    Blest emblem of Masonic art!

Let us be *true; the unerring Plumb,*
  Dropped from the unseen Master's hand,
Rich-fraught with truthfulness has come,
  To bid us rightly walk and stand;
    That the All-seeing Eye of God
    May bless us from the heavenly land.

Dear friend, whose generous heart I know,
  Whose virtues shine so far abroad,—
Long may you linger here below,
  To share what friendship may afford!
    Long may the Level, Plumb and Square,
    Speak forth by you the works of God.

ROB MORRIS

The three greatest moral forces are FAITH, which is the only true WISDOM, and the very foundation of all government; HOPE, which is STRENGTH, and insures success; and CHARITY, which is BEAUTY, and alone makes animated, united effort possible. These forces are within reach of all men; and an association of men, actuated by them, ought to exercise an immense power in the world. If Masonry does not, it is because she has ceased to possess them.

ALBERT PIKE

PEACE, UNITY AND PLENTY

Two pillars reared within God's house
    With wonder craftsmen scan,
And ponder o'er the symbols there
    Displayed by mystic plan.
Their chapiters by skill adorned
    With purity's design,
The lily's spotless petals show
    Unsullied grace, benign.

The network joining all its parts,
    With aptness typifies
The cords that form eternal bonds
    On which our strength relies.
The rare exuberance of seeds
    The pomegranate holds,
Denotes the plenteous supply
    Of good our plan unfolds.

May peace her influence extend
    Throughout the Mason's sphere
And craftsmen of the mystic art
    Her principles revere.
No strife engendered in her course,
    No wrongs to discord lead,
Where, with the Masons' firm support
    True peace shall reign indeed.

Where'er our brethren congregate,
　Whatever foes assail,
In vain attempt to mar their peace,
　May unity prevail.
Complete cohesion of the craft
　No rupture e'er shall see,
Where all, by mystic symbols taught,
　Are strong for unity.

May plenty, with her bounteous hand,
　E'er strew the Masons' way
Extending over each broad land
　In which they hold their sway.
In fervent prayer let each true heart
　With thanks to Him incline,
The Giver of each perfect gift,
　The Architect divine.

Peace, unity and plenty, then,
　The mystic craft shall bless,
As through symbolic search we seek
　The means of happiness.
The beauties of symbolic art,
　Evolved from ages past,
Shall then their excellence display
　And light the world at last.

LEWIS A. MCCONNELL

THE FIRE OF THE MIND

I solemnly declare that but for love of knowledge, I should consider
the life of the meanest hedger and ditcher, as preferable to that of the
greatest and richest man here present: for the fire of the mind is like
the fire which the Persians burn in the mountains,—it flames night and
day, and is immortal, and not to be quenched! . . .
　Love knowledge with a great love . . .
　Love that which, if you are rich and great, will sanctify the blind
fortune which made you so, and make men call it justice,—love that

which, if you are poor, will render your poverty respectable, and make the proudest feel it unjust to laugh at the meanness of your fortunes,—love that which will comfort you, adorn you, and never quit you,—which will open to you the kingdom of thought, and all the boundless regions of conception, as an asylum against the cruelty, the injustice and the pain that may be your lot in the outer world,—that which will make your motives habitually great and honourable, and light up in an instant a thousand noble disdains at the very thought of meanness and fraud!

Therefore, if any young man here has embarked his life in pursuit of knowledge, let him go on without doubting or fearing the event;—let him not be intimidated by the cheerless beginnings of knowledge, by the darkness, from which she springs, by the difficulties which hover around her, by the wretched habitations in which she dwells, by the want and sorrow which sometimes journeys in her train; but let him ever follow her as the Angel that guards him, and as the Genius of his life. She will bring him out at last into the light of day, exhibit him to the world comprehensive in acquirements, fertile in resources, rich in imagination, strong in reasoning, prudent and powerful above his fellows, in all the relations and in all the offices of life.

SYDNEY SMITH

A RIDDLE

There is a Mansion vast and fair,
  That doth on unseen pillars rest;
No Wanderer leaves the portals there,
  Yet each how brief a guest!
The craft by which that mansion rose,
  No thought can picture to the soul;
Tis lighted by a Lamp which throws
  Its stately shimmer through the whole.
As crystal clear, it rears aloof
The single gem which forms its roof,
And never have the eye surveyed
The Master who that Mansion made.

FRIEDRICH VON SCHILLER

So numerous indeed and so powerful are the causes, which serve to give a false bias to the judgement, that we, upon many occasions, see wise and good men on the wrong as well as on the right side of questions, of the first magnitude to society. This circumstance, if duly attended to, would furnish a lesson of moderation to those, who are ever so much persuaded of their being in the right, in any controversy.

ALEXANDER HAMILTON

THE LAYING OF THE CORNERSTONE

The symbol of a stalwart faith thou art,
  Firm set and sure, for ages there to stand,
  At once the token of a cunning hand,
And of the consecrated, faithful heart;
To those who follow us shalt thou impart
  Some knowledge of the tasks this day fulfilled,
  And of the men that wrought it, wise and skilled,
Their mem'ry shall thy presence ever start;
O stone, thou art an altar, on thee rears
  A Temple, standing wondrous in the sun,
A lesson unto all the coming years
  Of faithfulness to work today begun,
And on thee, raised in glory, there appears
  All Wisdom, Strength and Beauty, joined in one.

R. J. McLAUCHLIN

Through some unknown process of reasoning we have certain things that are called the Arts, and to be connected with them raises you above your fellow Man. Say, how do they get that way? If a Man happens to take up Painting and becomes only a mediocre painter, why should he be classed above the Bricklayer who has excelled every other Bricklayer? The Bricklayer is a true Artist in his line or he could not have achieved the top. The Painter has not been acclaimed the best in his line hence the Bricklayer is superior. Competition is just as keen in either line. In fact there are more good Bricklayers than Painters. If you are the best Taxi Driver you are as much an Artist as Kreisler. You save lives by your skilful driving. That's a meritorious profession, is it not?

WILL ROGERS

SOURCE

Seers seek for wisdom's flowers in the mind
    And write of symbols many a learned tome.
    (Grow roses still, though rooted in black loam.)
The mystic search earth till eyes go blind
For soul of roses, yet what use to find
    A spirit penned within a catacomb?
Nay, all they learn is weightless as sea-foam
That drifts from wave to wave upon the wind.

In rushes Cap and Bells! How very droll
    The ways of students and the foolish books;
    He finds no secrets of Freemason's art
In mind nor rose nor tomb nor musty scroll;
Where no wit is, where all loves are, he looks
And reads their hidden meaning in his heart.

CARL H. CLAUDY

Beauty is undoubtedly the signature of the master to the work into which he has put his soul; it is the divine spirit manifested. And to see it when it is not, to create it by the power of an inward look, is not that the highest reach of love?

HONORÉ DE BALZAC

The love of the beautiful calls man to fresh exertions, and awakens him to a more noble life; and the glory of it is, that as painters imitate, and poets sing, and statuaries carve, and architects rear up the gorgeous trophies of their skill,—as everything becomes beautiful, and orderly, and magnificent,—the activity of the mind rises to still greater, and to better, objects.

SYDNEY SMITH

ETERNAL BEAUTY

A thing of beauty is a joy forever:
Its loveliness increases; it will never
Pass into nothingness; but still will keep
A bower quiet for us, and a sleep
Full of sweet dreams, and health, and quiet breathing.

JOHN KEATS

If I had my life to live over again, I would have made a rule to read
some poetry and listen to some music at least once a week; for perhaps
the parts of my brain now atrophied would thus have been kept active
through use.

The loss of these tastes is a loss of happiness, and may possibly be
injurious to the intellect, and more probably the moral character, by
enfeebling the emotional part of our nature.

CHARLES DARWIN

THE BUILDING CODE

Our ancient brethren used their tools
With confidence and skill;
Though centuries have passed away,
Their works are standing still;
With admiration and with awe,
Our hearts and souls they thrill.

They called in Wisdom to conceive
And execute the plan;
Then Strength to make the structure sure
When first the work began;
Then Beauty to adorn and make
A monument to man:

So we, who build in later days,
Still use the self-same tools,
Still follow through the Master-Plan,
Still use the self-same rules,
Still work with diligence and skill,
As did the Ancient Schools;

Would use the Plumb for rectitude
As day by day goes by,
The Level to remind us all
That we must lowly be,
That right and true our work may prove
When we the Square apply;

No longer work with wood and stone,
But rather, with the mind
We would erect a dwelling-place
Wherein our souls may find
A quiet and a holy rest
At peace with all mankind;

And so, as we continually build
These dwellings for the soul,
Would work with Wisdom and with Strength,
Perchance to reach the goal;
Then crown our work with Beauty rare
To make the perfect whole.

MONTFORD C. HOLLEY

THE POEM OF TRATHEL

In an old Gaelic poem called "The Poem of Trathel," there is a scene
which pictures a mother playing a harp while her children gather
around, entranced as they listen to the sweet strains which issue from
the harp at her touch on the trembling strings. She stops. The music
ceases, and she lays down the harp. The children pick it up and finger
the strings in an attempt to reproduce the music which had come from
the harp at the touch of their mother's fingers. In vain. A confusion of

harsh discordant sounds comes forth but not the sweet music they longed to hear as a result of their own efforts. In bitter disappointment they cry out: "Oh Mother, why doesn't it answer us too? Show us the strings where the music is."

She replies, "My children, it is a secret I cannot tell you, nor can it be told except in the presence of Wisdom, Strength, and Beauty. Wisdom to discern the True, Strength to resist Error and Appreciation of Spiritual Beauty, qualities which you must acquire for yourselves. The music is in the strings, but the power to draw it out is not mine to give you. I can help, but you must seek and find it for yourselves. If you truly wish to acquire this power you can do so, but think not the task is easy. It will come when you have earned it, but only after long and patient search."

So it is with us. Our unaccustomed fingers wander among the wires of the harp of life. We seek the string where dwells the harmony of the soul. We seek the lost song, the lost chord, the lost word.

Yet after all it is not really lost. The sweet harmony is in the strings all the time. We must learn, by study and practice, the art of drawing it out. In like manner, the Word we call lost is near at hand, even in our own hearts. It is we ourselves who lack the power to recognize it. The harmony of the soul *is in* the harp of life, it is not lost, and we can acquire the power to draw it forth if we will only patiently seek and work for it.

This search for the harmony unheard by mortal ears, the harmony discerned only by the spiritual ear of the soul attuned to the divine strings of the heavenly harp, is the great purpose of Masonry. We call it the search for the Lost Word.

CHARLES CLYDE HUNT

It is only through the morning gate of the beautiful that you can penetrate into the realm of knowledge. That which we feel here as beauty we shall one day know as truth.

FRIEDRICH VON SCHILLER

The Fatherhood of God

The cornerstone of Freemasonry is the doctrine of the Fatherhood of God and the brotherhood of man and by the Holy Bible, the Great Light in Masonry, we are taught, "that of one blood made He all the nations of the earth." Masonry recognizes the right of every man to worship God freely and according to the dictates of his own conscience and in his own way and according to the forms and ceremonies of his choice.

ARTHUR S. TOMPKINS

THE LOVE OF GOD

Could you with ink the ocean fill,
    And were the sky of parchment made,
Were every stalk on earth a quill,
    And every man a scribe by trade,
To write the love of God above
    Would drain the ocean dry,
Nor would the scroll contain the whole
    Though stretched from sky to sky.

ANONYMOUS

DOUBT NOT THY FATHER'S CARE

O heart, when troubles come
Or grief is hard to bear,
Or hopes long-cherished fade,
Doubt not thy Father's care.

One certainty is sure;
One truth beyond compare:
God watches over you,
Doubt not thy Father's care.

GAIL BROOK BURKET

Oh that men would praise the LORD for his goodness,
  And for his wonderful works to the children of men!
For he satisfieth the longing soul,
  And filleth the hungry soul with goodness.
Such as sit in darkness and in the shadow of death,
  Being bound in affliction and iron;
Because they rebelled against the words of God,
  And contemned the counsel of the Most High:
Therefore he brought down their heart with labour;
  They fell down, and there was none to help.

  Then they cried unto the LORD in their trouble,
    And he saved them out of their distresses.
  He brought them out of darkness and the shadow of death,
    And brake their bands in sunder.

  Oh that men would praise the LORD for his goodness,
    And for his wonderful works to the children of men!

From PSALM CVII

I find daily life not always joyous, but always interesting. I have some sad days and nights, but none that are dull. As I advance deeper into the vale of years, I live with constantly increasing gusto and excitement. I am sure it all means something; in the last analysis, I am an optimist because I believe in God. Those who have no faith are quite naturally pessimists and I do not blame them.

WILLIAM LYON PHELPS

FATHERHOOD OF GOD

To the man who himself strives earnestly, God also lends a helping hand.

AESCHYLUS

Here is my Creed. I believe in one God, Creator of the Universe. That he governs it by his Providence. That he ought to be worshipped. That the most acceptable service we render him is doing good to his other children. That the soul of man is immortal and will be treated with justice in another life respecting its conduct in this.

BENJAMIN FRANKLIN

There is a kingdom on the earth, though it is not of it—a kingdom of wider bounds than the earth—wider than the sea and earth, though they were rolled together as finest gold and spread by the beating of hammers. Its existence is a fact as our hearts are facts, and we journey through it from birth to death without seeing it; nor shall any man see it until he has first known his own soul; for the kingdom is not for him, but for his soul. And in its dominion there is glory such as hath not entered imagination—original, incomparable, impossible of increase.

I do not understand myself. The most I am sure of is that I am doing a Master's will, and that the service is a constant ecstasy. When I think of the purpose I am sent to fulfil, there is in me a joy so inexpressible that I know the will is God's.

LEW WALLACE

GOD IS LOVE

God is love; his mercy brightens
  All the path in which we rove;
Bliss he wakes and woe he lightens;
  God is wisdom, God is love.

Chance and change are busy ever;
  Man decays, and ages move;
But his mercy waneth never;
  God is wisdom, God is love.

E'en the hour that darkest seemeth,
  Will his changeless goodness prove;
From the gloom his brightness streameth,
  God is wisdom, God is love.

He with earthly cares entwineth
  Hope and comfort from above;
Everywhere his glory shineth;
  God is wisdom, God is love.

JOHN BOWRING

... There is no truth more thoroughly established, than that there exists in the economy and course of nature an indissoluble union between virtue and happiness, between duty and advantage, between the genuine maxims of an honest and magnanimous policy, and the solid rewards of public prosperity and felicity.... The propitious smiles of Heaven can never be expected on a nation that disregards the eternal rules of order and right, which Heaven itself has ordained.

GEORGE WASHINGTON

OUR VOWS

In Mason's lodge with darkened eyes,
　And cable-tow about me,
I swore to hail all mysteries,
　That Masons keep and Masons prize;
All brothers' secrets whispered low,
　All words they speak and things they do,
In mystic manner taught me.

On yonder book, that oath I took,
　And I will break it never;
I'll stand by this, and this, and this,
　Forever and forever.

I swore to answer and obey
　All summons made me duly,
By brother hand or lodge array;
　I swore that I would never stray
From ancient laws and rules that bound
　Freemasons, in the days renowned,
But would observe them truly.

I'll stand by this, etc.

I swore in charity to care,
　For all in sorrow hidden;
My brother on the darkened square,
　His widow with dishevelled hair,
His sorrowing orphan, doomed to stray
　Upon a long and desolate way
While tears gush forth unbidden.

I'll stand by this, etc.

116

I swore to deal in honesty,
  With each true heart around me;
That honour bright, should always be
  Unbroken bond 'twixt him and me;
Nor guile, nor wrong, nor cruel fraud,
  Should break, or loose that holy cord
With which my vows have bound me.

I'll stand by this, etc.

I swore the chastity to shield
  Of woman true and tender;
Of Masons' widow, wife and child,
  His mother, sister undefiled;
Those pure and innocent, whose love
  Makes Masons' homes like heaven above,
I am the sworn defender.

I'll stand by this, etc.

I swore to guard the portals close
  To the Masonic Temple;
To purge the quarries of their dross,
  To build the mystic walls of those
In body perfect, honest heart,
  And mind mature in moral art,
By precept and example.

I'll stand by this, etc.

These were our vows; be these our care,
  And may such light be given,
In answer to our earnest prayer,
  That we may always do and dare
All that God's gracious laws enjoin;
  And so, as life's last shades decline
We may be found in Heaven.

On yonder book those vows we took,
  And let us break them never;
Let's stand by this, and this and this,
  Forever and forever.

Attributed to ROB MORRIS

I have faith in labour, and I see the goodness of God in placing us in a world where labour alone can keep us alive. I would not change, if I could, our subjection to physical laws, our exposure to hunger and cold, and the necessity of constant conflicts with the material world. I would not, if I could, so temper the elements that they should infuse into us only grateful sensations, that they should make vegetation so exuberant as to anticipate every want, and the minerals so ductile as to offer no resistance to our strength and skill.

WILLIAM ELLERY CHANNING

I see the marks of God in the heavens and the earth; but how much more in a liberal intellect, in magnanimity, in unconquerable rectitude, in a philanthropy which forgives every wrong, and which never despairs of the cause of Christ and human virtue: I do and I must reverence human nature.

WILLIAM ELLERY CHANNING

THE SOUL'S JOURNEY

Our birth is but a sleep and a forgetting:
The Soul that rises with us, our life's Star,
   Hath had elsewhere its setting,
      And cometh from afar:
   Not in entire forgetfulness,
   And not in utter nakedness,
But trailing clouds of glory do we come
   From God, who is our home:
Heaven lies about us in our infancy!
Shades of the prison-house begin to close
   Upon the growing Boy,
But he beholds the light, and whence it flows,
   He sees it in his joy;
The Youth, who daily farther from the east
   Must travel, still is Nature's Priest,
      And by the vision splendid
      Is on his way attended;
At length the Man perceives it die away,
And fade into the light of common day.

WILLIAM WORDSWORTH

Why should I wish to see God better than this day?
I see something of God each hour of the twenty-four, and each
    moment then,
In the faces of men and women I see God and in my own face in
    the glass,
I see letters from God dropped in the street, and every one is
    signed by God's name.

WALT WHITMAN

PIPPA'S SONG

The year's at the spring
And day's at the morn;
Morning's at seven;
The hillside's dew-pearled;
The lark's on the wing;
The snail's on the thorn;
God's in his heaven—
All's right with the world.

ROBERT BROWNING

The power of spiritual forces in the Universe—how active it is everywhere! Invisible to the eyes and impalpable to the senses, it is inherent
in all things, and nothing can escape its operation. It is a fact that there
are these forces which make men in all countries fast and purify themselves, and with solemnity of dress institute services of sacrifice and
religious worship. Like the rush of mighty waters, the presence of unseen Powers is felt, sometimes above us, sometimes around us.
    In the *Book of Songs* it is said:

            The presence of the Spirit:
            It cannot be surmised,
            How may it be ignored!

    Such is the evidence of things invisible that it is impossible to doubt
the spiritual nature of man.

CONFUCIUS

Farewell! a long farewell, to all my greatness!
This is the state of man: to-day he puts forth
The tender leaves of hope, to-morrow blossoms,
And bears his blushing honours thick upon him:
The third day comes a frost, a killing frost;
And,—when he thinks, good easy man, full surely
His greatness is a-ripening,—nips his root,
And then he falls, as I do. I have ventur'd,
Like little wanton boys that swim on bladders,
This many summers in a sea of glory,
But far beyond my depth: my high-blown pride
At length broke under me, and now has left me
Weary, and old with service, to the mercy
Of a rude stream, that must for ever hide me.
Vain pomp and glory of this world, I hate ye:
I feel my heart new open'd. O, how wretched
Is that poor man, that hangs on princes' favours!
There is, betwixt that smile we would aspire to,
That sweet aspect of princes, and their ruin,
More pangs and fear than wars or women have:
And when he falls, he falls like Lucifer,
Never to hope again. . . .
I know myself now: and I feel within me
A peace above all earthly dignities,
A still and quiet conscience. . . . Too much honour.
O! 'tis a burden, Cromwell, 'tis a burden,
Too heavy for a man that hopes for heaven.
And,—when I am forgotten, as I shall be,
And sleep in dull cold marble, where no mention
Of me more must be heard of,—say, I taught thee,
Say, Wolsey, that once trod the ways of glory,
And sounded all the depths and shoals of honour,
Found thee a way, out of his wrack, to rise in:
A sure and safe one, though thy master miss'd it.
Mark but my fall, and that that ruin'd me.
Cromwell, I charge thee, fling away ambition:
By that sin fell the angels; how can man then,
The image of his Maker, hope to win by't?
Love thyself last: cherish those hearts that hate thee;
Corruption wins not more than honesty.
Still in thy right hand carry gentle peace,
To silence envious tongues: be just, and fear not.

Let all the ends thou aim'st at be thy country's,
Thy God's and truth's: then, if thou fall'st,
Thou fall'st a blessed martyr. Serve the king;
And—Pry'thee lead me in:
There take an inventory of all I have,
To the last penny! 'tis the king's! my robe,
And my integrity to Heaven, is all
I dare now call my own.
Had I but serv'd my God with half the zeal
I serv'd my king, he would not in my age
Have left me naked to mine enemies.

WILLIAM SHAKESPEARE

IUDGE NOT

I remember that in time of childhood I was very religious: I rose
in the night, was punctual in the performance of my devotions, and
abstinent. One night I had been sitting in the presence of my father,
not having closed my eyes during the whole time, and with the
holy Koran in my embrace, whilst numbers around us were asleep.

I said to my father, "Not one of these lifteth up his head to perform
his genuflexions; but they are all so fast asleep that you would say
they are dead."

He replied, "Life of your father, it were better if thou also wert
asleep than to be searching out the fault of mankind. The boaster
sees nothing but himself, having a veil of conceit before his eyes. If
he were endowed with an eye capable of discerning God, he would
not discover any person weaker than himself."

SADI

FELLOWCRAFT'S SONG

His laws inspire our being—
    Our light is from His sun;
Beneath the Eye All-seeing,
    Our Mason's work is done;
His Plumbline in uprightness
    Our faithful guide shall be;
And in the Source of Brightness
    Our willing eyes shall see.

Thou, Father, art the Giver
  To every earnest prayer!
Oh, be the Guide forever
  To this, our Brother dear!
By law and precept holy,
  By token, word and sign,
Exhalt him, now so lowly
  Upon this Grand Design.

Within thy Chamber name him
  A Workman, wise and true!
While loving Crafts shall claim him
  In bonds of friendship due;
Thus shall the walls extol Thee,
  And future ages prove
What Masons ever call Thee,
  The God of Truth and Love!

ROB MORRIS

Let me recall a scene from one of the great books of the world, "War and Peace" by Count Leo Tolstoy. . . . One of the arresting figures of the story is Count Pierre Bezuhov. Pierre is the richest man in Russia, owning vast estates, including both the land and the serfs on the land. Like so many young noblemen of his day, he has lived a wild, sensual, dissolute life, careless alike of the rights and wrongs of his fellows. He was married to a beautiful, sensual woman, whose paramour he has just killed in a duel.

On his way to St. Petersburg he falls in with an old man, simply dressed, but with the light of a great peace in his face. The stranger addresses the Count and tells him he has heard of his misfortune, referring to the duel resulting in the death at his hands of the lover of his wife. He is aware, too, as he goes on to say, of the wild, sin-be-spattered life the Count has lived, of his way of thinking, of his pride, indolence, and ignorance. The Count listened to these severe words, he hardly knew why—perhaps because he heard in them an undertone of sympathy, the accent of a great pity, and what he heard in the voice he saw in the kindly face.

On the hand of the old man the Count noticed a ring. He asked the stranger if he was not a Mason. Whereupon the old man, looking searchingly into the eyes of the Count, said that he belonged to that order, in whose name he extended to him the hand of a brother man, in the name of God the Father.

A smile curled on the lips of the Count, who said, "I ought to tell you I do not believe in God."

The old Freemason smiled as a rich man, holding millions in his hand, might smile at a poor wretch.

"Yes, you do not know Him, sir," said the stranger. "You do not know Him, that is why you are unhappy. But He is here, He is within me, He is in thee, and even in these scoffing words you have just uttered. If He is not, we should not be speaking of Him, sir. Whom dost thou deny? How came there within thee the conception that there is such an incomprehensible Being?"

Something in the venerable stranger, who spoke earnestly, as one who stood in the light of a vision, touched the Count deeply, and stirred in him a longing to see what the old man saw and to know what he knew. Abject, hopeless, haunted by an ill-spent life, with the blood of a fellow man on his hands—his eyes betrayed his longing to know God. Though he did not speak, the kindly eyes of the stranger read his face and answered his unasked question, "He exists, but to know Him is hard. It is not attained by reason, but by life. The highest truth is like the purest dew. Can I hold in an impure vessel that pure dew and judge of its purity? Only by inner purification can we know Him."

Finally, the old man asked the young nobleman if he would not like to look into the mysteries of Masonry. Not so much what the stranger had said as what he was—his gentle, austere, benign spirit, that had in it something of the Fatherhood of God—made the Count say, "Yes."

The stranger asked him to report at a certain room in St. Petersburg, where he would be introduced to those high in authority among Freemasons. Meanwhile, what the gently stern old man had said sank into the soul of the hitherto heedless young nobleman; and when he reported at the lodge room and was asked, as every man is asked, the one indispensable question: "Do you believe in God?"—something deeper than his doubts, something higher than his skepticism spoke within him, and he answered, "Yes."

There follows a detailed description of his initiation, which those who are not Masons may be curious to read. Unfortunately, it tells them nothing of what takes place in a lodge room on such occasions; but it will show them the spirit that lives and glows on the altar of Masonry. No one but a Mason could have written it; and while the chain of evidence is not quite complete, I am safe in saying that, as with Count Pierre in the story, so with Count Tolstoy himself, it was Masonry which first lifted him out of the pit of atheism and sensualism, set his feet upon the Rock of Ages, and started him toward the city of God.

JOSEPH FORT NEWTON

THE BOOK OF BOOKS

Within this ample volume lies
The mystery of mysteries.
Happiest they of human race
To whom their God has given grace
To read, to fear, to hope, to pray,
To lift the latch, to force the way;
But better had they ne'er been born
That read to doubt or read to scorn.

SIR WALTER SCOTT

For God in giving life to all created things is surely bountiful to them according to their qualities. Hence the tree that is full of life He fosters and sustains, while that which is ready to fall He cuts off and destroys.

CONFUCIUS

THE ANVIL

I paused last eve beside the blacksmith's door,
    And heard the anvil ring, the vesper's chime,
And looking in I saw upon the floor
    Old hammers, worn with beating years of time.
"How many anvils have you had?" said I,
    "To wear and batter all these hammers so?"
"Just one," he answered. Then with twinkling eye:
    "The anvil wears the hammers out, you know."
And so, I thought, the anvil of God's Word
    For ages skeptics' blows have beat upon
But though the noise of falling blows was heard
    The anvil is unchanged; the hammers gone.

JOHN CLIFFORD

I have been driven many times to my knees by the overwhelming conviction that I had nowhere else to go. My own wisdom, and that of all about me seemed insufficient for the day.

ABRAHAM LINCOLN

I believe in a God—this is a fine, praiseworthy thing to say. But to acknowledge God wherever and however he manifests Himself, that in truth is heavenly bliss on earth.

JOHANN WOLFGANG VON GOETHE

Let us speak of the cause which led the Supreme Arranger of the universe to produce and regulate that universe. He was good; and he who is good has no kind of ill-will. Exempt from that, he willed that created things should be, as far as possible, like Himself.

PLATO

COMPELLED TO VALOUR BY OUR HERITAGE

O God, we pray Thy help in this dark hour
When we must face the evil forces hurled
With demon fury and tempestuous power
Against the righteous order of the world.

Undaunted by the tumult of our day,
Like patriots of old inspired by Thee,
We hold our onward course and periled way
That men may know the joys of liberty.

Oh, keep the vision ever in our mind
Of life according to Thy holy plan:
Our father, God, our brothers, all mankind,
And earth a habitation fit for man.
Compelled to valour by our heritage,
We sow our lives to yield that golden age.

GAIL BROOK BURKET

God is neither the object of sense, nor subject to passion, but invisible, only intelligible, and supremely intelligent. In his body he is like the *light*, and in his soul he resembles truth. He is the universal *spirit* that pervades and diffuseth itself over all nature. All beings receive their *life* from him. There is but one only God, who is not, as some are apt to imagine, seated above the world, beyond the orb of the universe; but being Himself all in all, he sees all the beings that fill his immensity; the only Principle, the *Light* of Heaven, the Father of all. He produces everything; He orders and disposes everything; He is the Reason, the Life, and the Motion of all being.

PYTHAGORAS

The Brotherhood of Man

Masonry is an international fraternity. Its members are prepared to travel in foreign countries and work and receive the wages of a Master Mason. Each is enjoined to be loyal to his own country, without hatred of other lands—knowing that other men love their countries as he loves his. In all the teaching of Masonry there is a recognition of the human race as a family, a brotherhood—a sense of the fact that the good of humanity as a whole does actually exist—and that is the one thing needed today. The world is perishing for lack of Brotherhood, and though we have the great ideal on our lips, it has not yet found its way into our hearts and hands.

JOSEPH FORT NEWTON

HANDS ACROSS THE SEA

Here's "Hands across the sea!" good sirs,
  here's "Hands across the sea!"
To every isle and continent
  where'er our brethren be;
For we are one in sympathy,
  as we are one in name;
The self-same tools are bright with use
  and mystic lights aflame;

The same designs on trestle-board
  by which our tasks are wrought,
Their symbol-truths impressed on heart
  and centered in our thought.
For that which counts for greatest good
  is through the lives of each,
Who by their acts exemplify
  the principles we teach.

The world's great heart is throbbing
  with the spirit of unrest;
We hear the cry that welleth up
  from peoples long oppressed;
We see the rule of mammon
  and the grasping hand of greed,
The travesties of justice
  and the toiler's bitter need,
The striving for the mastery,
  the ever-present fear,
With nation watching nation,
  and the war-clouds hovering near;

And the question ever riseth
  as portentous signs we trace,
What will the final outcome be,
  and what the saving grace?
And Masonry makes answer
  with its never-changing plan—
The Fatherhood of God,
  the Brotherhood of Man!

Though aeons upon aeons break
  upon the shores of time,
This is the grand fulfilment,
  and the prophesy sublime;
This is the work of trestle-board
  for brethren everywhere,
For never was there greater need
  for level, plumb and square,

For trowel with cement of love
  to strengthen and unite
The human race in brotherhood,
  and usher in the Light!
To all who aid this glorious work,
  wherever they may be,
Here's to the Craft in homeland,
  and here's "Hands across the sea!"

LAWRENCE N. GREENLEAF

128

It is not enough that in the lodge room or among Freemasons the bond of brotherhood should hold. It is the mission of the craft to spread the gospel of human kinship that all the world will acknowledge the bonds of amity and accord. Freemasonry is no longer an exclusive and withdrawn body, doing good by stealth or concerned only for its own. Its principles are blazoned for all men to behold; if now we fail to match fair professions with worthy deeds the fraternity will be brought into contempt and will deserve the condemnation of mankind.

ANONYMOUS

Above all things let us never forget that mankind constitutes one great brotherhood; all born to encounter suffering and sorrow, and therefore bound to sympathize with each other.

ALBERT PIKE

BROTHERHOOD

Speak well of every man you can:
    Think only thoughts of good;
Write splendid words about your friends;
    Thus hasten Brotherhood.

W. W. RILEY

He that saith he is in the light, and hateth his brother, is in darkness even until now. He that loveth his brother abideth in the light, and there is none occasion of stumbling in him. But he that hateth his brother is in darkness, and walketh in darkness and knoweth not whither he goeth, because that darkness hath blinded his eyes. . . . If a man say, I love God, and hateth his brother, he is a liar: for he that loveth not his brother whom he hath seen, how can he love God whom he hath not seen? And this commandment have we from him, That he who loveth God love his brother also.

I JOHN, 2:9-11; 4:20-21

ABOU BEN ADHEM

Abou Ben Adhem (may his tribe increase!)
Awoke one night from a deep dream of peace,
And saw, within the moonlight in his room,
Making it rich, and like a lily in bloom,
An Angel writing in a book of gold:
Exceeding peace had made Ben Adhem bold,
And to the Presence in the room he said,
"What writest thou?" The Vision raised its head,
And with a look made of all sweet accord
Answered, "The names of those who love the Lord."
"And is mine one?" said Abou. "Nay, not so,"
Replied the Angel. Abou spoke more low,
But cheerily still; and said, "I pray thee, then,
Write me as one that loves his fellow men."

The Angel wrote, and vanished. The next night
It came again with a great wakening light,
And showed the names whom love of God had blessed,
And, lo! Ben Adhem's name led all the rest!

LEIGH HUNT

One of the most impressive and touching things in human history is that certain ideal interests have been set apart as especially venerated among all peoples. Guilds have arisen to cultivate the interests embodied in art, science, philosophy, fraternity, and religion, to train men in their service, to bring their power to bear upon the common life of mortals and send through that common life the glory of the ideal, as the sun shoots its transfiguring rays through the great dull cloud, evoking beauty from the brown earth. Such is Masonry, which unites all these high interests and brings to their service a vast, world-wide fraternity of free men, built upon a basis of spiritual faith, whose mission it is to make men friends, to refine and exalt their lives, to turn them from the semblance of life to homage for truth, righteousness, and character. Forming one great society over the whole globe, it upholds every noble and redeeming ideal of humanity, making all good things better by its presence, like a meadow that rests on a subterranean stream. He who would reckon the spiritual possessions of our race must take account of the genius of Masonry and its ministry to the highest life of man.

JOSEPH FORT NEWTON

A CREED

There is a destiny that makes us brothers;
  None goes his way alone:
All that we send into the lives of others
  Comes back into our own.

I care not what his temples or his creeds,
  One thing holds firm and fast—
That into his fateful heap of days and deeds
  The soul of man is cast.

EDWIN MARKHAM

My country is the world; my countrymen are mankind.

WILLIAM LLOYD GARRISON

HOW GOOD AND HOW PLEASANT

Behold, how pleasant and how good
  For brothers such as we
In this united Brotherhood
  To dwell in unity.
'Tis like the oil on Aaron's head
  Which to his feet distills;
Like Hermon's dew so richly shed
  On Zion's sacred hills.

For there the Lord of light and love
  A blessing sent with power;
O, may we all this blessing prove,
  Even life forevermore.
On friendship's altar, rising here,
  Our hands now plighted be,
To live in love, with hearts sincere,
  In peace and unity.

GILES FONDA YATES

UNIVERSAL BROTHERHOOD

The idea of the universal brotherhood of all men is as profound as it is simple. We too easily assume that, because the idea is readily grasped, it is not profound; or, on an occasion when we glimpse some of the deeper meanings of the notion of brotherhood, we hastily avert our eyes lest we should be too shaken by the ethical insights of that moment. The demands upon personal and group conduct which the notion of brotherhood makes are fundamentally at variance with the demands made by racism. The belief in the Fatherhood of God and its necessary corollary, the brotherhood of man, is our greatest affirmative religious resource for attacking the caste system. Either God is the Father of all men or He is not. If we say he is not, we deny the Christian God and resort to some lesser pagan god of tribe or clan or race. That is what Hitler commanded his followers to do. If we accept the Fatherhood of God, we must accept the brotherhood of man.

B. G. GALLAGHER

MAN'S INHUMANITY TO MAN

Many and sharp the numerous ills
    Inwoven with our frame;
More pointed still, we make ourselves
    Regret, remorse and shame;
And man, whose heaven-erected face
    The smiles of love adorn,
Man's inhumanity to man,
    Makes countless thousands mourn.

ROBERT BURNS

Let us discard all this quibbling about this man and the other man, this race and that race and the other race, being inferior and therefore they must be placed in an inferior position. Let us discard all these things, and unite as one people throughout this land, until we shall once more stand up declaring that all men are created equal.

ABRAHAM LINCOLN

A MAN'S A MAN FOR A' THAT

Is there, for honest poverty,
   That hangs his head, and a' that?
The coward-slave, we pass him by,
   We dare be poor for a' that!
     For a' that, and a' that,
       Our toils obscure, and a' that;
     The rank is but the guinea stamp;
       The man's the gowd for a' that.

What tho' on hamely fare we dine,
   Wear hodden-grey, and a' that;
Gie fools their silks, and knaves their wine,
   A man's a man for a' that.
     For a' that, and a' that,
       Their tinsel show, and a' that;
     The honest man, tho' e'er sae poor,
       Is King o'men for a' that.

Ye see yon birkie, ca'd a lord,
   Wha struts, and stares, and a' that;
Tho' hundreds worship at his word,
   He's but a cuif for a' that:
     For a' that, and a' that,
       His riband, star, and a' that,
     The man of independent mind,
       He looks and laughs at a' that.

A prince can mak a belted knight,
   A marquis, duke, and a' that;
But an honest man's aboon his might,
   Guid faith he mauna fa' that!
     For a' that, and a' that,
       Their dignities, and a' that,
     The pith o' sense, and pride o' worth,
       Are higher rank than a' that.

Then let us pray that come it may,
As come it will for a' that;
That sense and worth, o'er a' the earth,
May bear the gree, and a' that.
For a' that and a' that,
It's coming yet, for a' that,
That man to man the warld o'er
Shall brothers be for a' that.

ROBERT BURNS

IDEAL LOVE

Love! love is the flight of the soul towards God; towards the great, the sublime, and the beautiful, which are the shadow of God upon earth. Love your family, the partner of your life, those around you ready to share your joys and sorrows; love the dead who were dear to you and to whom you were dear. But let your love be the love taught you by Dante and by us—the love of souls that aspire together; do not grovel on the earth in search of a felicity which it is not the destiny of the creature to reach here below; do not yield to a delusion which inevitably would degrade you into egotism. To love is to give and take a promise for the future. God has given us love, that the weary soul may give and receive support upon the way of life. It is a flower springing up on the path of duty; but it cannot change its course. Purify, strengthen, and improve yourselves by loving. Act always—even at the price of increasing her earthly trials—so that the sister soul united to your own may never need, here or elsewhere, to blush through you or for you. The time will come when, from the height of a new life, embracing the whole past and comprehending its secret, you will smile together at the sorrows you have endured, the trials you have overcome. . . .

Love humanity. You can only ascertain your own mission from the aim set by God before humanity at large. God has given you your country as cradle, and humanity as mother; you cannot rightly love your brethren of the cradle if you love not the common mother.

GIUSEPPE MAZZINI

He prayeth best, who loveth best
All things both great and small;
For the dear God who loveth us,
He made and loveth all.

THE MOTHER LODGE

There was Rundle, Station Master,
  An' Beazeley of the Rail,
An' 'Ackman, Commissariart,
  An' Donkin o' the jail;
An' Blake, Conductor-Sargent,
  Our Master twice was 'e,
With 'im that kept the Europe shop,
  Old Framjee Eduljee.

Outside—"Sergeant! Sir! Salute! Salaam!"
Inside—"Brother," an' it doesn't do no 'arm.
We met upon the Level an' we parted on the Square,
An' I was Junior Deacon in my Mother Lodge out there!

We'd Bola Nath, Accountant.
  An' Saul, the Aden Jew,
An' Din Mahammed, draughtsman
  Of the Survey Office, too;
There was Babu Chuckerbutty,
  An' Amir Singh the Sikh,
An' Castro from the fittin'-sheds,
  The Roman Catholick.

We 'adn't good regalia,
  An' our Lodge was old and bare,
But we knew the Ancient Landmarks,
  An' we kept them to a hair;
An' lookin' on it backwards
  It often strikes me thus,
There ain't such things as infidels,
  Excep', perhaps, it's us.

135

For monthly, after Labour,
  We'd all sit down and smoke,
(We dursn't give no banquits,
  Lest a brother's caste was broke),
An' man and man got talkin'
  Religion an' the rest,
An' every man comparin'
  Of the God 'e knew the best.

So man on man got talkin',
  An' not a brother stirred
Till mornin' waked the parrots
  An' that dam' brain-fever-bird;
We'd say 'twas 'ighly curious,
  An' we'd all ride 'ome to bed,
With Mo'amed, God, an' Shiva
  Changin' pickets in our 'ead.

Full oft on Gov'ment service
  This rovin' foot 'ath pressed,
An' bore fraternal greetin's
  To the Lodges east and west,
Accordin' as commanded
  From Kohat to Singapore,
But I wish that I might see them
  In my Mother Lodge once more!

I wish that I might see them,
  My Brethren black and brown,
With the trichies smellin' pleasant
  An' the hog-darn* passin' down;

An' the old khansamah† snorin'
  On the bottle-khana‡ floor,
Like a Master in good standing
  With my Mother Lodge once more!

Outside—"Sergeant! Sir! Salute! Salaam!"
Inside—"Brother," an' it doesn't do no 'arm.
We met upon the Level an' we parted on the Square,
An' I was Junior Deacon in my Mother Lodge out there!

*Cigar-lighter.   RUDYARD KIPLING
†Butler.
‡Pantry.

When a man is on the plains he sees the lowly grass and the mighty
pine tree and says, "How big is the tree and how small is the grass!"
But when he ascends the mountain and looks from its high peak on
the plain below, the mighty pine tree and the lowly grass blend into
one indistinguishable mass of green verdure. So in the sight of the
worldly there are differences of rank and position—one is a king,
another is a cobbler, one a father, another a son, and so on—but when
the divine sight is opened, all appear as equal and one, and there remains no distinction of good and bad, high and low.

SRI RĀMAKRISHNA

By the law of God, given by Him to humanity, all men are free, are
brothers, and are equals.

GIUSEPPE MAZZINI

THE TEMPLE

The Temple made of wood and stone may crumble and decay,
But there's a viewless fabric which shall never fade away,
Age after age each Mason strives to carry out his plan,
But still the work's unfinished which those ancient Three began.
None but immortal eyes may view complete in all its parts,
The Temple formed of Living Stones—the structure made of hearts.

*   *   *   *   *   *

'Neath every form of government, in every age and clime,
Amid the world's convulsions and the ghastly wrecks of time,
While empires rise in splendour and are conquered and o'erthrown,
And cities crumble in the dust, their very sites unknown.
Beneath the sunny smile of peace, the threatening frown of strife,
Lo! Masonry has stood unmoved—with age renewed her life.
She claims her votaries in all climes, for none are under ban,
Who place implicit trust in God, and love their fellow man.

137

The heart that shares another's woe, beats just as warm and true
Within the breast of Christian, or Mohammedan, or Jew.
She levels all distinctions from the highest to the least,
The Kings must yield obedience to the peasant in the East.

*   *   *   *   *   *

What honouréd names on history's page, o'er whose brave deeds we
    pore,
Have knelt before our sacred shrine, and trod the checkered floor!
Kings, princes, statesmen, heroes, bards, who squared their actions
    true,
Between the Pillars of the Porch, they pass in long review.
O brothers! what a glorious thought for us to dwell upon;
The mystic tie which binds our hearts, bound that of
    WASHINGTON.
Although our past achievements we with conscious pride review,
As long as there's Rough Ashlars there is work for us to do.
We still must shape the Living Stone with instrument of love,
For that eternal Mansion in the Paradise above.
Toil as we've toiled in ages past, to carry out the plan—
'Tis this: The Fatherhood of God, the Brotherhood of Man.

LAWRENCE N. GREENLEAF

The Masonic Fraternity is a single, indivisible fellowship which is neither divided nor affected by local or by national boundaries; like the sky it bends a single arch over the fifty or sixty countries in which it is at work, and that arch is nowhere broken into separate areas, nor does any country cut it into separate segments. A country is in the Fraternity, but the Fraternity is nowhere shut up inside a country. It has one set of Landmarks, one set of Degrees, one teaching for the whole world. It has a single membership, and it is into that membership that a man enters when he is made a Mason. Masons differ as men from one country to another, they use different languages, they have different religions, but *such differences* have nothing to do with their Freemasonry; it is everywhere self-same, one thing and one thing only, with single membership; its only boundaries are the boundaries of the world.

H. L. HAYWOOD

THE LEVEL AND THE SQUARE

We meet upon the Level
  and we part upon the Square;
What words of precious meaning
  those words Masonic are!
Come, let us contemplate them!
  they are worthy of a thought;
In the very walls of Masonry
  the sentiment is wrought.

We meet upon the Level,
  though from every station come,
The rich man from his palace
  and the poor man from his home;
For the rich must leave his wealth and state
  outside the Mason's door,
And the poor man finds his best respect
  upon the Checkered Floor.

We act upon the Plumb—
  'tis the orders of our Guide—
We walk upright in virtue's way
  and lean to neither side;
Th' All-Seeing Eye that reads our hearts
  doth bear us witness true,
That we still try to honour God
  and give each man his due.

We part upon the Square,
  for the world must have its due;
We mingle with the multitude,
  a faithful band and true;
But the influence of our gatherings
  in memory is green,
And we long upon the Level
  to renew the happy scene.

There's a world where all are equal—
　　we are hurrying towards it fast,
We shall meet upon the Level there,
　　when the gates of Death are passed;
We shall stand before the Orient,
　　and our Master will be there,
To try the blocks we offer
　　with His own unerring Square.

We shall meet upon the Level there,
　　but never thence depart;
There's a Mansion—'tis all ready
　　for each trusting, faithful heart—
There's a Mansion, and a Welcome,
　　and a multitude is there
Who have met upon the Level,
　　and been tried upon the Square.

Let us meet upon the Level, then,
　　while labouring patient here;
Let us meet and let us labour,
　　though the labour be severe;
Already in the western sky
　　the signs bid us prepare
To gather up our Working Tools
　　and part upon the Square.

Hands round, ye faithful Brotherhood,
　　the bright fraternal chain,
We part upon the Square below,
　　to meet in heaven again!
What words of precious meaning
　　those words Masonic are—
We meet upon the Level
　　and we part upon the Square.

ROB MORRIS

140

Let us at all times remember that all American citizens are brothers of a common country, and should dwell together in bonds of fraternal feeling.

ABRAHAM LINCOLN

ARE YOU A MAN?

I do not ask, my friend, if you
Were born a Gentile or a Jew,
A Buddhist, or Mohammedan:
I only ask, are you a man?

It matters not, my friend, to me
If you are black as black can be,
Or coloured red, or brown, or tan:
I ask but this, are you a man?

I care not, brother, whence you came,
Nor do I seek to know your name,
Your race, religion, creed or clan:
I want to know if you're a man.

I care not if you're homely quite,
Or handsome as an angel bright,
If you, throughout your little span,
Have only shown yourself a man.

I think that most men think like that:
They hate a weakling, loathe a rat;
They've always liked, since time began,
One who is first and last a man.

W. R. SHIELDS

Man should not live for himself alone, for he is a member of one great family or brotherhood, each member of which derives its support and assistance from the whole, and is therefore a dependent being. This dependence of the parts is true of all created matter, and is beautifully exemplified in all the works of the Sovereign Architect of the Universe, as proclaimed in the dignity, peace and harmony of nature . . .

J. Q. GOSS

JUST A LITTLE LODGE-ROOM

Just a quiet little lodge-room,
　But a mighty force for good;
With its loyal band of members
　Learning more of brotherhood;
Striving, stumbling, but progressing
　Down a pathway toward the right;
Just a humble bunch of plain folks,
　Reaching, seeking for the light.

Just a quiet little lodge-room,
　How it stirs the heart and soul
With the thrill of great endeavour
　Toward a high and common goal;
With each pledge of faith and courage
　To maintain the forward fight,
On the road that leads them onward
　Even onward to the light!

GEORGE B. STAFF

I'm quite sure that . . . I have no race prejudices, and I think I have no colour prejudices nor caste prejudices nor creed prejudices. Indeed, I know it. I can stand any society. All that I care to know is that a man is a human being—that is enough for me; he can't be any worse.

SAMUEL L. CLEMENS

A DAY OF THANKSGIVING

We are travelling East, my Brother,
   Whenever, in gratefulness,
We think of the things that every day brings
   Our lives and our homes to bless.
We are finding the Path, my Brother,
   Though frugal may be our feast,
If the good that we knew is the good that we do—
   Ah, then we are travelling East.

We are learning the Work, my Brother,
   Whenever, with kindly aim,
We lighten the care and our plenty we share
   With the poor and the halt and lame.
We are speaking the Word, my Brother,
   And finding our joys increased,
When we can bring cheer to replace a child's tear—
   Ah, then we are travelling East.

We are bringing the Light, my Brother,
   Whenever we greet a friend,
Whenever we lift a poor soul gone adrift,
   Or one in distress defend.
We are marking the Way, my Brother,
   When through us has sorrow ceased,
When something we've said to a lone heart has sped—
   Ah, then we are travelling East.

We are travelling East, my Brother,
   Whenever, in thankful mood,
We pause for a day to think and to pray,
   To set forth our gratitude.
The Word, the Work, my Brother,
   Through ages have never ceased—
With the Word that is true and the Word we can do,
   Ah, then we are travelling East.

WILBUR D. NESBIT

This is the challenge of these supreme times. The hope of a new world is alive today in millions of hearts the world around. May we not take courage from past achievements? No single one of us has passively accepted life; we have all insisted upon remaking it. Looked at from day to day little may seem to be accomplished, and yet what a series of victories a human being wins in a lifetime! . . .

And the record of the individual is magnified in the achievement of the race. Laboriously the progenitor of man separated himself off from the brutes. With indescribable slowness the scope of life was enlarged, its rude economy enriched by discovery and invention, and beautified by the rise and development of the arts. Gradually the periphery of interest in others was pushed out, so that whereas it was once inconceivable for man to be vitally concerned for the welfare of any one beyond the confines of his tribe, the time came when Terence could say: "I deem nothing alien to my feelings that concerns a human being."

MAX OTTO

ALWAYS A MASON

Let no king quite put off his crown:
    I still would have him kingly when
In some old inn the king sat down
    To banquet with his serving-men.
I love a mild and merry priest,
    Whom Brothers toast, and neighbours prod;
Yet I would have him, at the feast,
    A little of the man of God.

So with a Mason: I would see
    Him somewhat of a Mason still,
Though far from Lodge-rooms he may be,
    In court, or counting-house, or mill.
Whatever garment he may doff,
    What mark Masonic lay aside,
I would not have him quite put off
    The Craft he lately glorified.

A soldier is a soldier though
  He lays the sword aside awhile.
The time, the place, I do not know
  Man may not serve, or may not smile.
I know no moment anywhere,
  Whatever place the place may be,
A Mason may not always wear
  A little of his Masonry.

DOUGLAS MALLOCH

ECHOES

Fine men have walked this way before,
  Whatever Lodge your Lodge may be;
Whoever stands before the door,
  The sacred arch of Masonry,
Stands where the wise, the great, the good,
In their own time and place have stood.

You are not Brother just with these,
  Your friends and neighbours; you are kin
With Masons down the centuries;
  This room that now you enter in
Has felt the tread of many feet,
For here all Masonry you meet.

You walk the path the great have trod,
  The great in heart, the great in mind,
Who looked through Masonry to God,
  And looked through God to all mankind
Learned more than word or sign or grip,
Learned Man's and God's relationship.

To him who sees, who understands,
  How mighty Masonry appears!
A Brotherhood of many lands,
  A fellowship of many years,
A Brotherhood, so great, so vast,
Of all the Craft of all the past.

145

And so I say a sacred trust
  Is yours to share, is yours to keep;
I hear the voice of men of dust,
  I hear the step of men asleep;
And down the endless future, too,
Your own shall echo after you.

FRATERNITY

We build us temples tall and grand,
  With gifts we heap our altars high,
Unheeding how, on every hand,
  The hungry and the naked cry.
We sound our creeds in trumpet tone,
  With zeal we compass land and sea,
Unmindful of the sob and moan
  Of souls that yearn for sympathy.
We hurl to hell, we bear above,
  With equal ease we loose or bind,
Forgetful quite that God is Love,
  And Love is large and broad and kind.
O Thou Eternal Largeness, teach
  Our petty, shrivelled souls to swell
Till Thou, within their ampler reach,
  In every human heart may dwell;
Till Love alone becomes the creed
  Of every nation, tribe and clan,
The Fatherhood of God, indeed,
  The blessed Brotherhood of Man.

DAVID E. GUYTON

THE MYSTIC ART

The world may rail at Masonry,
  And scoff at Square and Line.
We'll follow with complacency
  The Master's great Design.

A king can make a gartered Knight
And breathe away another;
But he, with all his skill and might,
Can never make a Brother.

This power alone, thou Mystic Art,
Freemasonry, is thine:
The power to tame the savage heart
With brother-love divine!

EDWARD BULWER-LYTTON

Of no one age, Masonry belongs to all time; of no one religion, it finds great truths in all. Indeed, it holds that truth which is common to all elevating and benign religions, and is the basis of each; that faith which underlies all sects and over-arches all creeds, the sky above and the river bed below the flow of mortal years. It is not a religion, still less a cult, but it is a worship in which all good men may unite, that each may share the faith of all. It does not undertake to explain or dogmatically to settle those great mysteries which out-top human knowledge. Beyond the facts of faith it does not go. With the subtleties of speculation concerning these truths, and the unworldly envies growing out of them, it has not to do. There divisions begin, and Masonry was not made to divide men, but to unite them. It asks not for tolerance, but for fraternity, leaving each man free to think his own thought and fashion his own system of ultimate truth. Therefore, all through the ages it has been, and is today, a meeting place of differing minds and a prophecy of the final union of all reverent and devout souls.

JOSEPH FORT NEWTON

HE IS A MAN—MY BROTHER

What man soe'er I chance to see—
Amazing thought—is kin to me,
And if a man, my brother.

What though in silken raiment fine
His form be clad, while naked mine;
   He is a man, my brother.

What though with flashing chariot wheel
He spurn my cry, nor pity feel;
   He is a man, my brother.

What though he sit in regal state
And for an empire legislate,
   He is a man, my brother.

What though he grovel at my feet,
Spurned by the rabble of the street:
   He is a man, my brother.

What though his hand with crime be red,
His heart a stone, his conscience dead;
   He is a man, my brother.

And when we pass upon the street,
It is my brother that I meet;
   Alas, alas, my brother!

Though low his life, and black his heart,
There is a nobler, deathless part
   Within this man, my brother.

The soul which this frail clay enfolds
The image of his Maker holds—
   That makes this man my brother.

Though dimly there that image shine,
It marks the soul a thing divine,
   A child of God, my brother.

For him the spotless Son of God
The Perfect Man, our pathway trod,
  To show Himself our Brother.

Nor walks the earth so vile a wretch
But down to him that love doth stretch,
  As to an only brother.

Though deep the abyss with darkness lower,
'Tis but the measure of His power
  Who then will raise my brother.

A Saviour to the uttermost,
He will not see His brother lost,
  Nigh ruined, yet his brother.

HENRY NEHEMIAH DODGE

SONNET

So many men before thy Altars kneel
  Unthinkingly, to promise brotherhood;
  So few remain, humbly to kiss thy rood
With ears undeafened to thy mute appeal;
So many find thy symbols less than real,
  Their teachings mystic, hard to understand;
  So few there are, in all thy far-flung band
To hold thy banner high and draw thy steel,
  And yet—immortal and most mighty, thou!
  What hath thy lore of life to let it live?
  What is the vital spark, hid in thy vow?
Thy millions learned, as thy dear paths they trod,
  The secret of the strength thou hast to give;
"I am a way of common men to God."

CARL H. CLAUDY

My religion is very simple. I love God and all my brothers.

CHARLES RANN KENNEDY

As a little boy, I believed devoutly in a very personal God who listened to my every word and took a very personal interest in all of my activities. I actually talked to him a great deal. He was a God of love, but He was also a God of fierce and rapid justice. I felt as though His eyes were on me all of the time.

I was raised a Protestant, and as I look back I can see that somewhere along the line I learned to be suspicious of and condescending to all other sects. Then, at seventeen, during the first world war, I joined the Ambulance Service of the French Army and served for six months at Verdun. My friends were simple French soldiers. With one or two exceptions they were all Roman Catholics. I went to mass with them, carried them when wounded, saw them die. And I came to like them as people, to admire their courage, to respect their right to their faith, which was so different from my own.

Twenty years ago I began to make films about people all over the world. I took them as I found them—not as I wanted them to be. Wherever I went I soon discovered that when you break bread with people and share their troubles and joys the barriers of languages, of politics and of religion soon vanish. I liked them and they liked me. That was all that mattered.

I came to find that the peoples of this world have much more in common with one another than they have differences. I have found this true wherever I have gone—even in Moscow and the far reaches of Siberia. The most hardened Communist would eventually break down if you were kind to his children. This was true even though he knew he might be arrested the next day for becoming friendly with a foreigner.

As for the common man in Russia, my belief is that in spite of thirty-four years of Stalin and regimented thought control, he still loves his land and his church and his family. And he hates the cruelty of the secret police and the incredible stupidity of the Soviet bureaucrats. In fact, I believe that in a fundamental way he is very much like us; he wants to live his own life and be let alone.

All over the world I have watched the great religions in practice— Buddhist monks at their devotions in Manchuria—Shinto priests in their temples in Japan—and only last autumn the brave and hardy Serbian Moslems at their worship in Tito's Yugoslavia. I have come to hold a deep respect for all of man's great religions. And I have come to believe that despite their differences all men can worship side by side.

For myself, I believe in people—and in their given right to enjoy the freedoms we so cherish in America. I believe in justice and knowledge and decent human values. I believe in each man's right to a job and food and shelter. And I sincerely believe that one day all of these things will come to pass.

My real faith then is in a dream that, in spite of daily headlines prophesying man's destruction, we can build a better world, a world of peace and human brotherhood. Yes, even in our lifetime! This is my faith and my dream. In my small way I want to have a share in making it come about.

JULIEN BRYAN

THE LITTLE LODGE OF LONG AGO

The little Lodge of long ago—
It wasn't very much for show:
Men met above the village store,
And cotton more than satin wore,
And sometimes stumbled on a word,
But no one cared, or no one heard.
Then tin reflectors threw the light
Of Kerosene across the night
And down the highway served to call
The faithful to Masonic Hall.
It wasn't very much, I know,
The little Lodge of long ago.

But, men who meet in finer halls,
Forgive me if the mind recalls
With love, not laughter, doors of pine,
And smoky lamps that dimly shine,
Regalia tarnished, garments frayed,
Or cheaply bought or simply made,
And floors uncarpeted, and men
Whose grammar falters now and then—
For Craft, or Creed, or God Himself,
Is not a book upon a shelf:
They have a splendour that will touch
A Lodge that isn't very much.

It wasn't very much—and yet
This made it great: there Masons met—
And, if a handful or a host,
That always matters, matters most.
The beauty of the meeting hour
Is not a thing of robe or flow'r,
However beautiful they seem:
The greatest beauty is the gleam
Of sympathy in honest eyes.
A Lodge is not a thing of size,
It is a thing of Brotherhood,
And that alone can make it good.

DOUGLAS MALLOCH

The hunger for brotherhood is at the bottom of the unrest of the modern world.

GEORGE FREDERICK WATTS

BROTHERHOOD

The crest and crowning of all good,
Life's final star, is Brotherhood;
For it will bring again to earth
Her long-lost Poesy and Mirth;
Will send new light on every face,
A kingly power upon the race.
And till it comes, we men are slaves,
And travel downward to the dust of graves.

Come, clear the way, then, clear the way:
Blind creeds and kings have had their day.
Break the dead branches from the path:
Our hope is in the aftermath—
Our hope is in heroic men,
Star-led to build the world again.
To this event the ages ran:
Make way for Brotherhood—make way for Man!

EDWIN MARKHAM

Within the four seas every good man is a brother to us all.

THE NEW TRINITY

Three things must a man possess if his soul would live,
And know life's perfect good—
Three things would the all-supplying Father give—
Bread, Beauty and Brotherhood.

EDWIN MARKHAM

THE GREATNESS OF THE HUMBLE

Every man, in every condition, is great. It is only our own diseased sight which makes him little. A man is great as a man, be he where or what he may be. The grandeur of his nature turns to insignificance all outward distinctions. His powers of intellect, of conscience, of love, of knowing God, of perceiving the beautiful, of acting on his own mind, on outward nature, and on his fellow-creatures, these are glorious prerogatives . . . The truly great are to be found everywhere, nor is it easy to say, in what condition they spring up most plentifully. Real greatness has nothing to do with a man's sphere. It does not lie in the magnitude of his outward agency, in the extent of the effects which he produces. The greatest men may do comparatively little abroad. Perhaps the greatest in our city at this moment are buried in obscurity. Grandeur of character lies wholly in force of soul, in the force of thought, moral principles, and love, and this may be found in the humblest conditions of life.

WILLIAM ELLERY CHANNING

Charity and Benevolence

Masonic charity is strong, kindly, beautiful and tender, and not charity at all in the narrow sense of the word. Nay, it does not wait until a brother is in distress, but throw about him in his strength and prosperity the affectionate arm of friendship, without which life is cold and harsh. Friendship, fraternity, fellowship—this is the soul of Freemasonry, of which charity is but one gesture with a thousand meanings.

Freemasonry not only inculcates the principles of love and benevolence, it seeks to give them an actual and living presence in all the occupations and intercourse of life. It not only feels, it acts! It not only pities human suffering, it relieves it! Nowhere in the world can a good Mason feel himself alone, friendless or forsaken. The invisible but helpful arms of our Order surround him, wherever he may be. . . .

It is a common error to regard charity as that sentiment which prompts us to extend assistance to the unfortunate. Charity in a Masonic sense has a much broader meaning, and embraces affection and goodwill toward all mankind, but more especially our brethren in Freemasonry. It is this sentiment which prompts a Freemason to suffer long and be kind, to control his temper, forgive the erring, reach forth his hand to stay a falling brother, to warn him of his error and whisper in his ear that correction which his fault may demand, to close his ear to slander and his lips to reproach; in short, to do unto others as he would be done by.

Charity as applied to Freemasonry is different from the usual and accepted meaning. All true Masons meet upon the same level, regardless of wealth or station. In giving assistance we strive the too common error of considering charity only as that sentiment of commiseration which leads us to assist the poor and unfortunate with pecuniary donations. Its Masonic application is more noble and more extensive. We are taught not only to relieve a brother's material wants, the cry of hunger, etc., but to fellowship with him upon our own level, stripped of worldly titles and honours. When we thus appeal to him, giving spiritual advice, lifting him up morally and spiritually with no sense of humiliation to him, we set him free from his passion and wants. To such charity there is a reciprocity rich in brotherly love and sincere appreciation.

ANONYMOUS

Charity suffereth long, and is kind;
Charity envieth not;
Charity vaunteth not itself,
Is not puffed up,
Doth not behave itself unseemly,
Seeketh not her own,
Is not easily provoked,
Thinketh no evil;
Rejoiceth not in iniquity,
But rejoiceth in the truth;
Beareth all things,
Believeth all things,
Hopeth all things,
Endureth all things.
Charity never faileth.

I CORINTHIANS 13:4-8

Freemasonry has tenets peculiar to itself. They serve as testimonials of character and qualifications, which are only conferred after due course of instruction and examination. These are of no small value; they speak a universal language, and act as a passport to the attention and support of the initiated in all parts of the world. They cannot be lost as long as memory retains its power. Let the possessor of them be expatriated, shipwrecked or imprisoned, let him be stripped of everything he has got in the world, still those credentials remain, and are available for use as circumstances require. The good effects they have produced are established by the most incontestable facts of history. They have stayed the uplifted hand of the destroyer; they have softened the asperities of the tyrant; they have mitigated the horrors of captivity; they have subdued the rancour of malevolence; and broken down the barriers of political animosity and sectarian alienation. On the field of battle, in the solitudes of the uncultivated forest, or in the busy haunts of the crowded city, they have made men of the most hostile feelings, the most distant regions, and diversified conditions, rush to the aid of each other, and feel a special joy and satisfaction that they have been able to afford relief to a Brother Mason.

BENJAMIN FRANKLIN

What though a man win wealth and the applause of fame, and have not Charity, it is nothing; what though he sway the world with his eloquence and miss the high prize of "self-knowledge, self-reverence and self-control," even if men erect an obelisk of gold above his grave it is a monument to a failure. He only is wise who lives a simple, sincere, faithful life, building on the Square by the Plumb, toiling in the light of Eternity.

JOSEPH FORT NEWTON

The *state of human* existence is such that men are in some respects dependent on each other in many if not all relations in civilized life. As they have mutual wants, and stand in need of mutual assistance, no one can be placed in absolute independence of circumstances. Each individual, in the midst of all his affluence, is still dependent. Hence arise those mutual obligations by which not only the members of a neighbourhood or society, but the citizens of a nation and the inhabitants of the world are bound mutually to subserve each other's interest and promote each other's happiness.

This obligation corresponds with the very nature and fitness of things, and is necessarily binding on all mankind. But notwithstanding its nature, multitudes of the human family seldom feel its force, or comply with its requisitions. Hence, the unfortunate sufferer often wanders through the world, unpitied and forlorn. There are unfortunate sufferers, and such there will be till the end of time. Notwithstanding all human foresight, prudence and provident care, individuals are exposed, in numerous ways, to be suddenly precipitated from a state of affluence to penury and want. Hence, the virtuous citizen may be thrown into circumstances in which he shall have a just claim for charitable assistance. It is the glory of a nation or society to have its citizens or members kindly disposed, mutually to rejoice or sympathize together. A charitable disposition, in the view of the world, marks a character of true benevolence and worth, and draws kind benediction on the memory.

Charity is a shining virtue, adorns our nature, comports with the feelings of humanity, and is deeply characteristic of true benevolence of heart. Hence Masonry, as a charitable Institution, aside from all other considerations, is justly entitled to the approbation of mankind. Individuals, in their private capacity, are never expected promptly to meet all the exigencies of innocent sufferers. Hence, the union of individuals will afford the more sure means of effecting this important object.

If charity to the destitute is a duty, and a charitable society a blessing to the country, then the Masonic Institution *deserves* the patronage of every benevolent, humane, and charitable person, and the applause of mankind in general, as a useful and important Institution. It is a wise, a universal and a permanent establishment. Not circumscribed, as to charitable donations, by country, or confined to nation, sect, age or condition, it considers all mankind the children of one common parent, and brethren in one great family. It shields from danger, and on some degrees will even feed an enemy at the point of a sword, should his necessities absolutely require it. Such charity is God-like. It forgives an enemy, and renders good for evil. It covers a multitude of faults. Such benevolent charity disarms the heart of all enmity and, if universally exercised, would restore and perpetuate universal peace to the world. Hence the principles of Speculative Freemasonry, in every shape, when carried into practice, aim directly at the alleviation of human misery, the advancement of the peace, the harmony and happiness of society, and the friendship and brotherly affections of all the inhabitants of the earth.

SALEM TOWN

AS WE GO

In the battle of life
  We find sorrow and strife,
But there's happiness too, every day—
  If we stop by the road
Just to lighten the load
  Of the fellow who falls by the way.

He has days when the light
  Of the sun isn't bright—
Dark clouds bank up heavy and black;
  Greet this chap who is sad,
With a smile—make him glad—
  Chase his frown with a slap on the back.

SO

When we meet neighbour Brown,
  If he thinks he is down,
Let's help him along without boast;
  For the fellow who knows
That he reaps as he sows
  Is the fellow who smiles the most.

J. D. G.

There is a duty to the living more important than any charity to the dead.

EDGAR ALLAN POE

THE GOOD WORD

Our brother—aye, he is our friend;
 We do not hold the right to chide,
To flout and damn, world without end,
 The foibles that the past should hide.
Deep hidden in his heart of hearts,
 Or maybe shining forth alone
Is the good trait. Our censure smarts
 And sears till it is overthrown—
  Speak the good word!

Speak the good word—the word that gives
 The newer impulse and the hope,
A word that helps, and grows, and lives
 A Light to them that blindly grope
Through all the darkness of despair.
 They know their faults, and know them well!
Of censurings they have their share—
 The kind words are the ones that tell:
  Speak the good word!

A good word is a helping hand,
 A coin that's minted of fine gold;
To read the rote of faults we've banned
 May loose the eager climber's hold.
Our life is short; we cannot do
 All we would have it comprehend,
But this much, truly, I and you
 May do each day for this our friend—
  Speak the good word!

WILBUR D. NESBIT

THE LODGE ROOM OVER
SIMPKINS' STORE

The plainest lodge room in the land was over Simpkins' store,
Where Friendship Lodge had met each month for fifty years or more;
When o'er the earth the moon, full orbed, had cast her brightest
    beams,
The brethren came from miles around on horseback and in teams;
And O! what hearty grasp of hand, what welcome met them there,
As mingling with the waiting groups they slowly mount the stair,
Exchanging fragmentary news or prophecies of crop,
Until they reach the Tyler's room and current topics drop.
To turn their thoughts to nobler themes they cherish and adore,
And which were heard in meeting night up over Simpkins' store.

To city eyes, a cheerless room, long usage had defaced;
The tell-tale lines of lath and beam on wall and ceiling traced;
The light from oil-fed lamps was dim and yellow in its hue;
The carpet once could pattern boast, though now 'twas lost to view.

The altar and the pedestals that marked the stations three,
The gate-post pillars topped with balls, the rude-carved letter G,
Where village joiners clumsy work, with many things beside,
Where beauty's lines were all effaced and ornament denied;
There could be left no lingering doubt, if doubt there was before,
The plainest lodge room in the land was over Simpkins' store.

While musing thus on outward form the meeting time drew near,
And we had glimpse of inner life through watchful eye and ear;
When lodge convened at gavel's sound with officers in place,
We looked for strange, conglomerate work, but could no errors trace.

The more we saw, the more we heard, the greater our amaze,
To find those country brethren there so skilled in Masons' ways;
But greater marvels were to come before the night was through,
Where unity was not mere name, but fell on heart like dew;
Where tenents had the mind imbued, and truth's rich fruitage bore,
In plainest lodge room in the land, up over Simpkins' store.
To hear the record of their acts was music to the ear;
We sing of deeds unwritten which on angel's scroll appear;
A widow's case—four helpless ones—lodge funds were running low;
A dozen brethren sprang to feet and offers were not slow.

Food, raiment, things of needful sort, while one gave a load of wood,
Another shoes for little ones, for each gave what he could.
They spake the last: "I haven't things like those to give—but then
Some ready money may help out"—and he laid down a ten.
Were brother cast on darkest square upon life's checkered floor,
A beacon light to reach the white—was over Simpkins' store.

Like scoffer who remained to pray, impressed by sight and sound,
The faded carpet 'neath our feet was now like holy ground;
The walls that had such dingy look were turned celestial blue;
The ceiling changed to canopy where stars were shining through;
Bright tongues of flame from altar leaped, the G was vivid blaze;
All common things seemed glorified by heaven's reflected rays.
O! wondrous transformation wrought through ministry of love—
Behold the Lodge Room Beautiful!—fair type of that above.
The vision fades—the lesson lives! and taught as ne'er before,
In plainest lodge room in the land, up over Simpkins' store.

LAWRENCE N. GREENLEAF

The happiness of love is in action; its test is what one is willing to do for others.

LEW WALLACE

Oh, many a shaft, at random sent,
Finds mark the archer little meant!
And many a word, at random spoken,
May soothe or wound a heart that's broken!

SIR WALTER SCOTT

NOT WHAT WE GIVE

Not what we give, but what we share,
    For the gift without the giver is bare:
Who gives himself with his alms feeds three,
    Himself, his hungering neighbour, and Me.

JAMES RUSSELL LOWELL

CHARITY

There is so much good in the worst of us,
And so much bad in the best of us,
That it ill behoves any of us
To find fault with the rest of us.

ANONYMOUS

CHARITY

The Greatest of the Three

"Now, there abideth faith, hope, charity, these three." This was the expression made, in unusually poetic mood, by a master of the human mind: "These three, but the greatest of these is charity!"

The soul serene, impenetrably just,
Is first in CHARITY; we love to muse
On such a model; knit in strictest bonds
Of amity with spirits like disposed;
Aiming at truth for her own sake, this man
Passes beyond the golden line of Faith,
Passes beyond the precious line of Hope,
And sets his foot unmoved on CHARITY.
"A soul so softly radiant and so white,
The track it leaves seems less of fire than light."

ROB MORRIS

I SHALL NOT PASS THIS WAY AGAIN

Through this toilsome world, alas!
Once and only once I pass;
If a kindness I may show,
If a good deed I may do
To a suffering fellow man,
Let me do it while I can.
No delay, for it is plain
I shall not pass this way again.

ANONYMOUS

YOU MAY COUNT THAT DAY

If you sit down at set of sun
  And count the acts that you have done,
  And, counting, find
One self-denying deed, one word
That eased the heart of him who heard—
  One glance most kind,
That fell like sunshine where it went—
Then you may count that day well spent.

But if, through all the livelong day,
You've cheered no heart, by yea or nay—
  If, through it all
You've nothing done that you can trace
That brought the sunshine to one face—
  No act most small
That helped some soul and nothing cost—
Then count that day as worse than lost.

GEORGE ELIOT

WISHING

Do you wish the world were better?
  Let me tell you what to do.
Set a watch upon your actions,
  Keep them always straight and true.
Rid your mind of selfish motives,
  Let your thoughts be clean and high.
You can make a little Eden
  Of the sphere you occupy.

Do you wish the world were wiser?
  Well, suppose you make a start,
By accumulating wisdom
  In the scrapbook of your heart;
Do not waste one page on folly;
  Live to learn, and learn to live.
If you want to give men knowledge
  You must get it, ere you give.

Do you wish the world were happy?
  Then remember day by day
Just to scatter seeds of kindness
  As you pass along the way,
For the pleasures of the many
  May be ofttimes traced to one.
As the hand that plants an acorn
  Shelters armies from the sun.

ELLA WHEELER WILCOX

RULE FOR LIVING

Do all the good you can,
By all the means you can,
In all the ways you can,
In all the places you can,
At all the times you can,
To all the people you can,
As long as ever you can.

JOHN WESLEY

JUST THIS MINUTE

If we're thoughtful, just this minute,
  In whatever we say and do,
If we put a purpose in it
  That is honest through and through,
We shall gladden life and give it
  Grace to make it all sublime;
For, though life is long, we live it
  Just a minute at a time.

Yesterday is gone; to-morrow
  Never comes within our grasp;
Just this minute's joy or sorrow,
  That is all our hands may clasp.
Just this minute, let us take it
  As a pearl at precious price,
And with high endeavour make it
  Fit to shine in paradise.

STANLEY G. KETCHAM

If you really want to help your fellow-men, you must not merely have in you what would do them good if they should take it from you, but you must be such a man that they can take it from you. The snow must melt upon the mountain and come down in a spring torrent, before its richness can make the valley rich.

PHILLIPS BROOKS

QUESTION NOT

Question not, but live and labour,
 Till your goal be won,
Helping every feeble neighbour,
 Seeking help from none;
Life is mostly froth and bubble,
 Two things stand like stone—
Kindness in another's trouble,
 Courage in our own.

ADAM LINDSAY GORDON

GOOD DEEDS

How far that little candle throws his beams!
So shines a good deed in a naughty world.
Heaven doth with us as we with torches do;
Not light them for themselves; for if our virtues
Did not go forth of us, 'twere all alike
As if we had them not.

WILLIAM SHAKESPEARE

Begin the morning by saying to thyself, I shall meet with the busy-body, the ungrateful, arrogant, deceitful, envious, unsocial. All these things happen to them by reason of their ignorance of what is good and evil. But I who have seen the nature of the good that is beautiful, and of the bad that is ugly, and the nature of him who does wrong, that it is akin to me, not [only] of the same blood or seed, but that it participates [in the same] intelligence and [the same] portion of the divinity, I can neither be injured by any of them, for no one can fix on me what is ugly, nor can I be angry with my kinsmen, nor hate him. For we are made for cooperation, like feet, like hands, like eyelids, like the rows of the upper and lower teeth. To act against one another then is contrary to nature, and it is acting against one another to be vexed and to turn away.

MARCUS AURELIUS

WHAT MAKES A MASON?

What makes you a Mason, O brother of mine?
It isn't the dueguard, nor is it the sign,
It isn't the jewel which hangs on your breast,
It isn't the apron in which you are dressed,
It isn't the step, nor the token, nor grip,
Nor lectures that fluently flow from the lip,
Nor yet the possession of that mystic word
On five points of fellowship duly conferred.
Though these are essential, desirable, fine,
They don't make a Mason, O brother of mine.

That you to your sworn obligation are true—
'Tis that, brother mine, makes a Mason of you.
Secure in your heart you must safeguard your trust,
With lodge and with brother be honest and just,
Assist the deserving who cry in their need,
Be chaste in your thought, in your word and your deed,
Support him who falters, with hope banish fear,
And whisper advice in an erring one's ear.
Then will the Great Lights on your path brightly shine,
And you'll be a Mason, O brother of mine.

Your use of life's hours by the gauge you must try,
The gavel to vices with courage apply;
Your walk must be upright, as shown by the plumb,
On the level, to bourn whence no travellers come;
The Book of your faith be the rule and the guide,
The compass your passions shut safely inside;
The stone which the Architect placed in your care
Must pass the strict test of His unerring square,
And then you will meet with approval divine,
And you'll be a Mason, O brother of mine.

GEORGE H. FREE

Masonic charity is not limited to simple gifts and contributions of money or other tangible material of worldly goods, although these, when necessary, are right and proper, and are included within the term of charity. . . . True charity extends to *all* the wants of the great brotherhood of man. Have the cold and pitiless storms of a selfish, unfeeling world beat upon the heart, charity throws around it her broad mantle of brotherly love and affection, which warms and infuses into its whole being new life and animation, and as the genial showers and summer sun cause the face of nature to smile and look glad, so the drops of genial affection and the rays of brotherly love, beaming from its benign countenance of one whose heart is prompted by the honest impulses of genuine charity, cause the soul of the recipient thereof to overflow with gratitude and joy . . . The true Mason is continually seeking opportunities for the exercise of those virtues—the principles of Brotherly Love, Relief, and Truth—of Faith, Hope and Charity. . . . He knows his duties, and knowing seeks to reduce them to practice; for with him Masonry is a living *reality* and not *theory* alone. It is the practice of those virtues that he delights for he has learned that in doing good there is much joy. Is a brother afflicted and distressed, his hand is ever ready to aid and assist him, and to relieve his wants and necessities. The blessed influences of brotherly love and charity—twin daughters of Heaven—prompt him to those noble deeds of benevolence which give joy and gladness to many a weary, sad and sorrowing heart. . . . This is the charity which envieth not another and which puffeth not itself, which is kind and forbearing, full of long-suffering, and goodness and truth.

J. Q. GOSS

LOOK UP

Look up and not down.
Look forward and not back.
Look out and not in.
Lend a hand.

EDWARD EVERETT HALE

There is nothing that makes us love a man so much as praying for
him; and when you can once do this sincerely for any man, you have
fitted your soul for the performance of everything that is kind and
civil towards him. This will fill your heart with a generosity and
tenderness, that will give you a better and sweeter behaviour than anything that is called fine breeding and good manners. By considering
yourself as an advocate of God for your neighbours and acquaintance,
you would never find it hard to be at peace with them yourself. It
would be easy for you to bear with and forgive those for whom you
particularly implored the divine mercy and forgiveness.

WILLIAM LAW

Doing an injury puts you below your enemy; revenging one makes
you even with him; forgiving one sets you above him.

BENJAMIN FRANKLIN

THREE WORDS OF STRENGTH

There are three lessons I would write,
   Three words, as with a burning pen,
In tracings of eternal light,
   Upon the hearts of men.

Have hope. Though clouds environ round
  And gladness hides her face in scorn,
Put off the shadow from thy brow;
  No night but hath its morn.

Have faith. Where'er thy bark is driven—
  The calm's disport, the tempest's mirth—
Know this: God rules the hosts of heaven,
  The inhabitants of earth.

Have love. Not love alone for one,
  But man, as man, thy brother call;
And scatter, like a circling sun,
  Thy charities on all.

FRIEDRICH VON SCHILLER

WHAT OF YOUR MASONRY?

What of your Masonry? Is it put by,
Doffed with your apron, forgotten, to lie
Dormant and void, inefficient and vain,
Till in the lodge you resume it again?

Listen, my brother, true Masonry dwells
Out in the world, not in dungeons and cells;
It feeds the hungry, defends the oppressed,
Lifts those that languish, and soothes the distressed.

Masonry's place is in shop, street and store,
Fully as much as behind the tiled door.
'Tis not a thing to be hidden away,
It should be worn, used and lived day by day.

Worthy is study and labour to gain
Ritual skill, and perfection attain,
Yet this is only the means to an end,
Useful alone for the aid it can lend.

What of the lessons by Masonry taught?
Have you their practical principles caught?
Live by them, grow by them, build by them, too,
Let them your thought and your actions imbue.

GEORGE H. FREE

NEEDED: GOOD SAMARITANS

Open your eyes and look for some man, or some work for the sake
of men, which needs a little time, a little friendship, a little sympathy,
a little sociability, a little human toil. Perhaps it is a lonely person, or
an embittered person, or an invalid, or some unfortunate inefficient,
to whom you can be something. It may be an old man or it may be a
child. Or some good work is in want of volunteers who will devote a
free evening to it or will run on errands for it. Who can reckon up all
the ways in which that priceless fund of impulse, man, is capable of
exploitation! He is needed in every nook and corner. Therefore search
and see if there is not some place where you may invest your humanity.
Do not be put off if you find that you have to wait and to experiment.
Be sure that you will have disappointments to endure. But do not be
satisfied without some side line in which you may give yourself out
as a man to men. There is one waiting for you if only you are willing
to take it up in the right spirit.

ALBERT SCHWEITZER

A MASON

A Mason's hand is a hand that helps,
    That lifts the fallen one,
That comes, in need, with a kindly deed
    To him whose strength is gone.

A Mason's heart is a heart that loves
    The best that is good and true;
He stands the friend, his best to lend,
    Under his banner blue.

169

A Mason's eye is an eye that smiles
    And his a cheering voice;
He spreads the light, dispels the night
    And makes the world rejoice.

Over the earth in stranger lands,
    Where distant peoples dwell,
The eye, the grip, the life, the lip,
    Of love unchanging tell.

CARL W. MASON

Truth and Justice

No truth, for such is the nature of truth itself, can be any man's private property, or be owned or monopolized by anybody; it is in its own essence something free, something which any man can have who desires to have it. . . . Truth is one of the three Principal Tenets of Freemasonry . . . There are many truths *in* Freemasonry, some of them were first discovered and stated by Freemasons, but not one of them is the exclusive property of Freemasonry, because *no* truth can be anybody's private property; and the mere fact that a truth is found *in* Freemasonry cannot mean that it differs from the same truth when found outside it; and if a truth is found outside Freemasonry, in any religion, in any science, in any country, Freemasons know themselves to be as free to know and to use it as they may desire to. Then Truth as one of the Principal Tenets is not a philosophic idea, or a scientific idea, but is an ethical idea, and this idea means that any righteous man will never try to make any truth his own property or the property of his own fraternity, or church, or party, will never lay hands on any truth to distort it or to misrepresent it to gain something for himself or his party, and will never try to prevent any other man from having any truth. This is what a righteous man does about truth; he will keep it wholly free, he will never do violence to it, he will never misrepresent it, and he will never try to keep any other man from having it.

H. L. HAYWOOD

Truth must be loved for its own sake, but error is adopted and maintained because it suits the purpose of certain sets of people to keep the rest as much as possible in ignorance. To guard yourself against prejudice, you must be careful not to be peremptory in your judgment of things. It requires a great deal of time and experience to come to a right comprehension on certain subjects, therefore you must be slow in coming to a decision till you have opportunities of knowing better. Learn something every day, and think often on what you have learned;

by this you will gradually form your mind to embrace truth, from whatever quarter it may come.

WILLIAM FREND

TRUTH AND BEAUTY

Love of truth shows itself in this, that a man knows how to find and value the good in everything.

JOHANN WOLFGANG VON GOETHE

BE TRUE

Thou must be true thyself,
   If thou the truth wouldst teach;
Thy soul must overflow, if thou
   Another's soul wouldst reach!
It needs the overflow of heart
   To give the lips full speech.

Think truly, and thy thoughts
   Shall the world's famine feed;
Speak truly, and each word of thine
   Shall be a fruitful seed;
Live truly, and thy life shall be
   A great and noble creed.

HORATIUS BONAR

Truth never yet fell dead in the streets; it has such affinity with the soul of man, the seed however broadcast will catch somewhere and produce its hundredfold.

THEODORE PARKER

The knowledge of my own position and my own relations to the world, is truth. Thus every one may have his own truth, and yet it is the same truth.

JOHANN WOLFGANG VON GOETHE

Stand therefore, having your loins girt about with truth, and having on the breastplate of righteousness; and your feet shod with the preparation of the gospel of peace; above all, taking the shield of faith, wherewith ye shall be able to quench all the fiery darts of the wicked. And take the helmet of salvation, and the sword of the Spirit, which is the word of God.

EPHESIANS 6:14-17

The universe is to be valued because there is truth in it and beauty in it; and we live to discover the truth and the beauty no less than to do what is right. Indeed, we cannot attain to that state of mind in which we shall naturally do what is right unless we are aware of the truth and the beauty of the universe.

A. CLUTTON-BROCK

To believe your own thought, to believe that what is true for you in your private heart is true for all men—that is genius. Speak your latent conviction, and it shall be the universal sense; for always the inmost becomes the outmost—and our first thought is rendered back to us by the trumpets of the Last Judgment.

RALPH WALDO EMERSON

Truth, after all, wears a different face to everybody, and it would be too tedious to wait till all were agreed. She is said to lie at the bottom of a well, for the very reason, perhaps, that whomever looks down in search of her sees his own image at the bottom, and is persuaded not only that he has seen the goddess, but that she is far better-looking than he had imagined.

JAMES RUSSELL LOWELL

Are we disposed to be of the number of those who, having eyes, see not, and having ears, hear not the things which so nearly concern their temporal salvation? For my part, whatever anguish of spirit it might cost, I am willing to know the whole truth; to know the worst and to provide for it.

PATRICK HENRY

There is but one necessity, the Truth; that is why there is but one might, the Right. Advantage gained without Truth or Right is an illusion. Tyrants are short-sighted and make that mistake. Successful foul play seems to them a victory, but this victory is full of bitter ashes; the criminal believes that his crime is his accomplice; this is all wrong; his crime is his avenger; the murderer never fails to hurt himself with his own knife; treachery always betrays the traitor; the culprits, without expecting it, are collared by the invisible specter of their offence; an unworthy deed never lets you go. . . .

VICTOR HUGO

TRUTH, CRUSHED TO EARTH

Truth, crushed to earth, shall rise again—
The eternal years of God are hers;
But Error, wounded, writhes in pain,
And dies among his worshippers.

WILLIAM CULLEN BRYANT

With as deep a reverence for the True as ever inspired the bosom of man, I would, nevertheless, limit in some measure its modes of inculcation. I would limit to enforce them. I would not enfeeble them by dissipation. The demands of Truth are severe; she has no sympathy with the myrtles. All that is so indispensable in a Song, is precisely all that with which she has nothing whatever to do. It is but by making her a flaunting paradox to wreathe her in gems and flowers. In enforcing a truth we need severity rather than efflorescence of language. We must be simple, precise, terse. We must be cool, calm, unimpassioned. In a word, we must be in that mood, which, as nearly as possible, is the exact converse of the poetical. He must be blind, indeed, who does not perceive the radical and chasmal differences between the truthful and the poetical modes of inculcation. He must be theory-mad beyond redemption who, in spite of these differences, shall still persist in attempting to reconcile the obstinate oils and waters of Poetry and Truth.

EDGAR ALLAN POE

174

Truth must be sought for. It is not an entity lying outside us, like a boulder on the path, but a living and changing thing, which must evermore be possessed anew . . . Each man must win it for himself, such is the law, for it is not a commodity which can be handed by one man to another, though there are countless ways in which we can help each other find the light.

H. L. HAYWOOD

I say every man is to be a student, a thinker. This does not mean that he is to shut himself within four walls, and bend his body and mind over books. Men thought before books were written, and some of the greatest thinkers never entered what we call a study. Nature, Scripture, society, and life, present perpetual subjects for thought; and the man who collects, concentrates, employs his faculties on any of these subjects for the purpose of getting the truth, is so far a student, a thinker, a philosopher, and is rising to the dignity of a man. It is time that we should cease to limit to professed scholars the titles of thinkers, philosophers. Whoever seeks truth with an earnest mind, no matter when or how, belongs to the school of intellectual men.

WILLIAM ELLERY CHANNING

You will hear every day the maxims of a low prudence. You will hear that the first duty is to get land and money, place and name. "What is this Truth you seek? what is this Beauty?" men will ask, with derision. If, nevertheless, God have called any of you to explore truth and beauty, be bold, be firm, be true. When you shall say: "As others do, so will I; I renounce, I am sorry for it, my early visions; I must eat the good of the land and let learning and romantic expectations go, until a more convenient season;"—then dies the man in you; then once more perish the buds of art, and poetry, and science, as they have died already in a thousand thousand men.

RALPH WALDO EMERSON

It is not always needful for truth to take a definite shape; it is enough if it hovers about us like a spirit and produces harmony; if it is wafted through the air like the sound of a bell, grave and kindly.

JOHANN WOLFGANG VON GOETHE

It is also most true, that Truth is a Divine attribute and the foundation of every virtue. To be true, and to seek to find and learn the Truth, are the great objects of every good Mason.

ALBERT PIKE

Truth is the law of God. Acquired truth is the law of man. He who intuitively apprehends truth is one who, without effort, hits what is right, and without thinking understands what he wants to know; whose life is easily and naturally in harmony with the moral law. Such a one is what we call a saint or a man of divine nature. He who acquires truth is one who finds out what is good and holds fast to it.

In order to acquire truth, it is necessary to obtain a wide and extensive knowledge of what has been said and done in the world; critically to inquire into it; carefully to ponder over it; clearly to sift it; and earnestly to carry it out.

Thus absolute truth is indestructible. Being indestructible, it is eternal. Being eternal it is self-existent. Being self-existent, it is infinite. Being infinite, it is vast and deep. Being vast and deep, it is transcendental and intelligent. It is because it is vast and deep that it contains all existence. It is because it is infinite and eternal that it fulfills or perfects all existence. In vastness and depth it is like the Earth. In transcendental intelligence it is like Heaven. Infinite and eternal, it is the Infinite itself.

Such being the nature of absolute truth, it manifests itself without being seen; it produces effects without motion; it accomplishes its ends without action.

CONFUCIUS

THE OBJECT OF MASONRY

Flattering as it may be to the human mind, and truly honourable as it is to receive from our fellow citizens testimonies of approbation for exertions to promote the public welfare, it is not less pleasing to know that the milder virtues of the heart are highly respected by a Society whose liberal principles must be founded in the immutable laws of truth and justice.

To enlarge the sphere of social happiness is worthy of the benevolent design of a Masonic institution; and it is most fervently to be wished that the conduct of every member of the Fraternity, as well as those publications that discover the principles which actuate them, may tend to convince mankind that the great object of Masonry is to promote the happiness of the human race.

GEORGE WASHINGTON

SELF-ESTIMATE

I do not know what I may appear to the world; but to myself I seem to have been only like a little boy playing on the seashore, and diverting myself in it, now and then finding a smoother pebble or a prettier shell than ordinary, whilst the great ocean of truth lay all undiscovered before me.

SIR ISAAC NEWTON

From OF TRUTH

Truth, which only doth judge itself, teacheth, that the inquiry of Truth, which is the love-making, or wooing of it; the knowledge of Truth, which is the presence of it; and the belief of Truth, which is the enjoying of it; is the sovereign good of human nature. The first creature of God, in the works of the days, was the light of the sense; the last, was the light of reason; and His Sabbath work, ever since, is the illumination of His spirit. First He breathed light, upon the face, of the matter or chaos; then He breathed light, into the face of man; and still He breatheth and inspireth light, into the face of His chosen. The poet, that beautified the sect, that was otherwise inferior to the rest, saith yet excellently well: It is a pleasure to stand upon the shore, and to see ships tost upon the sea: a pleasure to stand in the window of a castle, and to see a battle, and the adventures thereof, below: but no pleasure is comparable, to the standing, upon the vantage ground of Truth: (a hill not to be commanded, and where the air is always clear, and serene;) and to see the errors, and wanderings, and mists, and tempests, in the vale below: so always, that this prospect, be with pity, and not with swelling, or pride. Certainly, it is Heaven upon earth, to have a man's mind move in charity, rest in providence, and turn upon the poles of Truth.

FRANCIS BACON

Everyman seeks for truth; but God only knows who has found it. It is, therefore, as unjust to persecute, as it is absurd to ridicule, people for those several opinions, which they cannot help entertaining upon the conviction of their reason. It is the man who tells, or who acts a lie, that is guilty, and not he who honestly and sincerely believes the lie. I really know nothing more criminal, more mean, and more ridiculous than lying. It is the production either of malice, cowardice, or vanity; and generally misses of its aim in every one of these views; for lies are always detected sooner or later. If I tell a malicious lie, in order to affect any man's fortune or character, I may indeed injure him for some time; but I shall be sure to be the greatest sufferer myself at last; for as soon as ever I am detected (and detected I most certainly shall be), I am blasted for the infamous attempt; and whatever is said afterward, to the disadvantage of that person, however true, passes for calumny. . . . Remember, then, as long as you live, that nothing but strict truth can carry you through the world, with either your conscience or your honour unwounded. It is not only your duty, but your interest; as a proof of which you may always observe, that the greatest fools are the greatest liars. For my own part, I judge of every man's truth by his degree of understanding.

LORD CHESTERFIELD

For it is to him who masters our minds by the force of truth, and not to those who enslave them by violence, that we owe our reverence.

VOLTAIRE

Justice in no wise consists in meting out to another that exact measure of reward or punishment which we think and decree his merit, or what we call his crime, which is more often merely his error, deserves. The justice of the father is not incompatible with forgiveness by him of the errors and offences of his child. The Infinite Justice of God does not consist in meting out exact measures of punishment for human frailties and sins. We are too apt to erect our own little and narrow notions of what is right and just, into the law of justice, and to insist that God shall adopt that as His law; to measure off something with our own little tapeline, and call it God's law of justice. Continually we

178

seek to ennoble our own ignoble love of revenge and retaliation, by misnaming it justice.

Justice to others and ourselves is the same; we cannot define our duties by mathematical lines ruled by the square, but must fill them with the great circle traces by the compasses; the circle of humanity is the limit, and we are but the point in its centre, the drops in the great Atlantic, the atom or particle, bound by a mysterious law of attraction which we term sympathy to every other atom in the mass; the physical and moral welfare of others cannot be indifferent to us; we have a direct and immediate interest in the public morality and popular intelligence, in the wellbeing and physical comfort of the people at large. The ignorance of the people, their pauperism and destitution, and consequent degradation, their brutalization and memoralization, are all diseases; and we cannot rise high enough above the people, nor shut ourselves up from them enough, to escape the miasmatic contagion and the great magnetic currents.

Justice is peculiarly indispensable to nations. The unjust State is doomed of God to calamity and ruin. This is the Eternal Wisdom and of history. "Righteousness exalteth a nation; but wrong is a reproach to nations." "The Throne is established by Righteousness. Let the lips of the Ruler pronounce the sentence that is Divine; and his mouth do no wrong in judgement!" The nation that adds province to province by fraud and violence, that encrouches on the weak and plunders its wards, and violates its treaties and the obligations of its contracts, and for the law of honour and fair-dealing substitutes the exigencies of greed and the base precepts of policy and craft and the ignoble tenets of expediency, is predestined to destruction; for here, as with the individual, the consequences of wrong are inevitable and eternal.

A sentence is written against all that is unjust, written by God in the nature of man and in the nature of the universe, because it is in the nature of the Infinite God. No wrong is really successful. The gain of injustice is a loss; its pleasure, suffering. Iniquity often seems to prosper, but its success is its defeat and shame. If its consequences pass by the doer, they fall upon and crush his children. It is a philosophical, physical, and moral truth, in the form of a threat, that God visits the iniquity of the fathers upon the children, to the third and fourth generation of those who violate His laws. After a long while, the day of reckoning always comes, to nation as to individual; and always the knave deceives himself, and proves a failure.

It is natural, when we are wronged, to desire revenge; and to persuade ourselves that we desire it less for our own satisfaction than to prevent a repetition of the wrong, to which the doers would be encouraged by immunity coupled with the profit of the wrong. To submit to be cheated is to encourage the cheater to continue; and we are apt to regard ourselves as God's chosen instruments to inflict His vengeance, and for Him and in His stead to discourage wrong by making it fruitless and its punishment sure. Revenge has been said to be "a kind of wild justice;" but it is always taken in anger, and therefore is unworthy of a great soul, which ought not to suffer its equanimity to be disturbed by ingratitude or villainy. The injuries done us by the base are as much unworthy of our angry notice as those done us by the insects and the beasts, and when we crush the adder, or slay the wolf or hyena, we should do it without being moved to anger, and with no more feeling of revenge than we have in rooting up a noxious weed.

And if it be not in human nature not to take revenge by way of punishment, let the Mason truly consider that in doing so he is God's agent, and so let his revenge be measured by justice and tempered by mercy. The law of God is, that the consequences of wrong and cruelty and crime shall be their punishment. Always, also, it remains true, that it is more noble to forgive than to take revenge.

ALBERT PIKE

Observe good faith and justice towards all Nations. Cultivate peace and harmony with all.—Religion and Morality enjoin this conduct; and can it be, that good policy does not equally enjoin it?—It will be worthy of a free, enlightened, and, at no distant period, a great nation, to give to mankind the magnanimous and too novel example of a People always guided by an exalted justice and benevolence.

GEORGE WASHINGTON

I have only one stone in my sling, but that stone is a good one; that stone is justice.

VICTOR HUGO

Truth is tough. It will not break, like a bubble, at a touch; you may kick it about all day, like a football, and it will be round and full at evening.

OLIVER WENDELL HOLMES

While craving justice for ourselves, it is never wise to be unjust to others. To deny valour in the enemy we have conquered is to underrate our victory; and if the enemy be strong enough to hold us at bay, much more to conquer us, self-respect bids us seek some other explanation of our misfortunes than accusing him of qualities inferior to our own.

There is no wiser providence than that our occupations, however rude or bloody, cannot wear us out morally; that such qualities as justice and mercy, if they really possess us, continue to live on under them, like flowers under the snow.

LEW WALLACE

It is better that acts of injustice occur than that they be redressed by unjust means.

It is better for you to suffer injustice than for the world to be without law. Therefore let everyone submit to the law.

JOHANN WOLFGANG VON GOETHE

Fortitude

Fortitude is not only physical courage in the face of "any pain, peril or danger" but moral courage; the strength to make a decision which may have undesirable consequences, because it is right; the venturesomeness and audacity to fly in the face of all accepted standards because it seems right.

So considered, fortitude becomes what its inner Masonic meaning intends, a foundation stone of character.

CARL H. CLAUDY

THE SOURCE OF PERSONAL POWER

Fortitude and faith are the words. That is what keeps a man going when he seems defeated. Believe that if you put your trust in God and keep at things with unremitting energy and intelligence you, too, can build a solid foundation beneath you upon which you may mount up to victory. Therefore, train your mind never to accept the thought of defeat about anything. That verse from the Bible makes an unbeatable inspiration in any situation: "If God be for us, who can be against us?" Hold it habitually in mind and it will train you to believe in yourself by constantly reminding you that you have extra power available.

NORMAN VINCENT PEALE

The soul little suspects its own courage. We have had to tear men's bodies to pieces, to burn, crush, strangle and crucify them to find that last wonderful drop of courage. Take even a common man, the commonest, and beat and bruise him enough and you will see his soul rise God-like.

FRANK CRANE

JUST BEING HAPPY

Just being happy is a fine thing to do.
Look on the bright side rather than the blue.
    Sad or sunny musing
    Is largely in your choosing,
While just being happy is a brave work and true.

Just being happy helps other souls along.
Their burdens may be heavy and they not strong.
    Your own skies will lighten
    If other skies you brighten
By just being happy with a heart full of song.

JOHN B. CRAFT

A BROTHER AS PILOT

When the charm of life is fading,
    And its joys are fleeing fast;
When the tempest gathers o'er thee
    And thy every bliss seems past.
Faint not then tho' thou art weary,
Mark the gold in yonder sky,
Friend the glorious days are coming,
    They are coming by and by.

What tho' now the flowers are drooping
    And the thorns oppress thee sore,
Tho' those scenes that once gave gladness
    Have a charm for thee no more,
Languish not, thy ills are transient,
    Let not tears bedim thine eyes,
For the glorious days are coming,
    They are coming by and by.

Fret not thou when darksome shadows
   Shall obscure life's little day,
And thou'lt find the bliss was nigh thee,
   Flit before thy gaze away.
Bravely on, meet them and conquer,
   Not sit idly down and sigh,
For the glorious days are coming,
   They are coming by and by.

What tho' friends erstwhile adored thee
   May forget that thou art here,
And shall spurn thy supplication
   When thou fain wouldst have their cheer.
Up and on, brave heart, nor falter,
   Neath misfortune scorn to lie,
For the glorious days are coming,
   They are coming by and by.

H. MACPHERSON

MUSIC

As battle weary men long for the sea
   Like tired children, seeking Mother's breast,
   And in its restless endlessness find rest,
Its crashing surf a soothing systole;
As seeks the storm-tossed ship the harbour's lee,
So mariners upon life's deep, hard-pressed
   To weather boiling trough and mounting crest,
Steer for the shelter of Freemasonry.

Her ancient waves of sound lap on the strand
   A melody more God's than man's. We hear,
   Like gentle murmurs in a curved sea shell
Which whispers of some far off wonderland
   Where lightning flashes from blue skies and clear,
   The rolling thunder of the ritual.

CARL H. CLAUDY

CAN YOU SING A SONG?

Can you sing a song to greet the sun,
    Can you cheerily tackle the work to be done,
Can you vision it finished when only begun,
    Can you sing a song?

Can you sing a song when the day's half through,
When even the thought of the rest wearies you,
With so little done and so much to do,
    Can you sing a song?

Can you sing a song at the close of the day,
When weary and tired, the work's put away,
With the joy that it's done the best of the pay,
    Can you sing a song?

JOSEPH MORRIS

WORTH WHILE

It is easy enough to be pleasant,
    When life flows by like a song,
But the man worth while is one who will smile,
    When everything goes dead wrong.
For the test of the heart is trouble,
    And it always comes with the years,
And the smile that is worth the praises of earth,
    Is the smile that shines through tears.

It is easy enough to be prudent,
    When nothing tempts you to stray,
When without or within no voice of sin
    Is luring your soul away;
But it's only a negative virtue
    Until it is tried by fire,
And the life that is worth the honour on earth,
    Is the one that resists desire.

By the cynic, the sad, the fallen,
  Who had no strength for the strife,
The world's highway is cumbered today,
  They make up the sum of life.
But the virtue that conquers passion,
  And the sorrow that hides in a smile,
It is these that are worth the homage on earth
  For we find them but once in a while.

ELLA WHEELER WILCOX

Resolved, never to do anything which I should be afraid to do if it were the last hour of my life.

JONATHAN EDWARDS

Be strong and of a good courage. Be not afraid; neither be thou discouraged; for I, the Lord thy God, am with thee withersoever thou goest.

JOSHUA I:9

INVICTUS

Out of the night that covers me,
  Black as the Pit from pole to pole,
I thank whatever gods may be
  For my unconquerable soul.

In the fell clutch of circumstance
  I have not winced nor cried aloud.
Under the bludgeonings of chance
  My head is bloody, but unbowed.

Beyond this place of wrath and tears
  Looms but the Horror of the shade,
And yet the menace of the years
  Finds and shall find me unafraid.

186

It matters not how strait the gate,
How charged with punishments the scroll,
I am the master of my fate:
I am the captain of my soul.

WILLIAM ERNEST HENLEY

THE ATHLETE'S PRAYER

Dear Lord, in the battle that goes on through life,
I ask but a field that is fair;
A chance that is equal with all in the strife,
And courage to strive and to dare.
And if I should win, let it be by the code,
With my faith and my honour held high;
And if I should lose, let me stand by the road
And cheer as the winner goes by.

ANONYMOUS

PRAYER

I do not ask to walk smooth paths
Nor bear an easy load.
I pray for strength and fortitude
To climb the rock strewn road.

Give me such courage I can scale
The hardest peaks alone
And transform every stumbling block
Into a stepping stone.

GAIL BROOK BURKET

JUDGMENT

Before God's footstool to confess
A poor soul knelt, and bowed his head;
"I failed," he cried. The Master said,
"Thou didst thy best—that is success!"

ANONYMOUS

DON'T QUIT

When things go wrong, as they sometimes will,
When the road you're trudging seems all up hill,
When the funds are low and the debts are high,
And you want to smile, but you have to sigh,
When care is pressing you down a bit,
Rest, if you must—but don't you quit.

Life is queer with its twists and turns,
As everyone of us sometimes learns,
And many a failure turns about
When he might have won had he stuck it out;
Don't give up, though the pace seems slow—
You might succeed with another blow.

Often the goal is nearer than
It seems to a faint and faltering man,
Often the struggler has given up
When he might have captured the victor's cup.
And he learned too late, when the night slipped down,
How close he was to the golden crown.

Success is failure turned inside out—
That silver tint of the clouds of doubt—
And you never can tell how close you are,
It may be near when it seems afar;
So stick to the fight when you're hardest hit—
It's when things seem worst that you mustn't quit.

ANONYMOUS

HOW DO YOU TACKLE YOUR WORK?

How do you tackle your work each day?
  Are you scared of the job you find?
Do you grapple the task that comes your way
  With a confident, easy mind?
Do you stand right up to the work ahead
  Or fearfully pause to view it?
Do you start to toil with a sense of dread
  Or feel that you're going to do it?

You can do as much as you think you can,
  But you'll never accomplish more;
If you're afraid of yourself, young man,
  There's little for you in store.
For failure comes from the inside first,
  It's there if we only knew it,
And you can win, though you face the worst,
  If you feel that you're going to do it.

Success! It's found in the soul of you,
  And not in the realm of luck!
The world will furnish the work to do,
  But you must provide the pluck.
You can do whatever you think you can,
  It's all in the way you view it.
It's all in the start you make, young man:
  You must feel that you're going to do it.

How do you tackle your work each day?
  With confidence clear, or dread?
What to yourself do you stop and say
  When a new task lies ahead?
What is the thought that is in your mind?
  Is fear ever running through it?
If so, just tackle the next you find
  By thinking you're going to do it.

EDGAR A. GUEST

SEE IT THROUGH

When you're up against a trouble,
  Meet it squarely, face to face;
Lift your chin and set your shoulders,
  Plant your feet and take a brace.
When it's vain to try to dodge it,
  Do the best that you can do;
You may fail, but you may conquer,
  See it through!

Black may be the clouds about you
And your future may seem grim,
But don't let your nerve desert you;
Keep yourself in fighting trim.
If the worse is bound to happen,
Spite of all that you can do,
Running from it will not save you,
See it through!

Even hope may seem but futile,
When with troubles you're beset,
But remember you are facing
Just what other men have met.
You may fail, but fall still fighting;
Don't give up, whate'er you do;
Eyes front, head high to the finish.
See it through!

EDGAR A. GUEST

COURAGE

A great deal of talent is lost in the world for want of a little courage.
Every day sends to their graves obscure men whom timidity prevented
from making a first effort; who, if they could have been induced to
begin, would in all probability have gone great lengths in the career of
fame. The fact is, that to do anything in the world worth doing we
must not stand back shivering and thinking of the cold and danger,
but jump in and scramble through as well as we can. It will not do to
be perpetually calculating risks and adjusting nice chances; it did very
well before the Flood, when a man would consult his friends upon an
intended publication for a hundred and fifty years, and live to see
his success afterwards; but at present, a man waits, and doubts, and
consults his brother, and his particular friends, till one day he finds
he is sixty years old and that he has lost so much time in consulting
cousins and friends that he has no more time to follow their advice.

SYDNEY SMITH

LIFE AND DEATH

So he died for his faith. That is fine—
    More than most of us do.
But stay, can you add to that line
    That he lived for it, too?

In death he bore witness at last
    As a martyr to truth.
Did his life do the same in the past
    From the days of his youth?

It is easy to die. Men have died
    For a wish or a whim—
From bravado or passion or pride.
    Was it harder for him?

But to live: every day to live out
    All the truth that he dreamt,
While his friends met his conduct with doubt,
    And the world with contempt—

Was it thus that he plodded ahead,
    Never turning aside?
Then we'll talk of the life that he led—
    Never mind how he died.

ERNEST H. CROSBY

PLAYING THE GAME

Life is a game with a glorious prize,
    If we can only play it right.
It is give and take, build and break,
    And often it ends in a fight;
But he surely wins who honestly tries
    (Regardless of wealth or fame),
He can never despair who plays it fair—
    How are you playing the game?

Do you wilt and whine, if you fail to win
  In the manner you think your due?
Do you sneer at the man in case that he can
  And does, do better than you?
Do you take your rebuffs with a knowing grin?
  Do you laugh tho' you pull up lame?
Does your faith hold true when the whole world's blue?
  How are you playing the game?

Get into the thick of it—wade in, boys!
  Whatever your cherished goal;
Brace up your will till your pulses thrill,
  And you dare—to your very soul!
Do something more than make a noise;
  Let your purpose leap into flame
As you plunge with a cry, "I shall do or die,"
  Then you will be playing the game.

ANONYMOUS

KEEP ON KEEPIN' ON

If the day looks kinder gloomy
And your chances kinder slim,
If the situation's puzzlin'
And the prospect's awful grim,
If perplexities keep pressin'
Till hope is nearly gone,
Just bristle up and grit your teeth
And keep on keepin' on.

Frettin' never wins a fight
And fumin' never pays;
There ain't no use in broodin'
In these pessimistic ways;
Smile just kinder cheerfully
Though hope is nearly gone,
And bristle up and grit your teeth
And keep on keepin' on.

There ain't no use in growlin'
And grumblin' all the time,
When music's ringin' everywhere
And everything's a rhyme.
Just keep on smilin' cheerfully
If hope is nearly gone,
And bristle up and grit your teeth
And keep on keepin' on.

ANONYMOUS

When the One Great Scorer comes to write against
your name—
He marks—not that you won or lost—but how you
played the game.

GRANTLAND RICE

MY WAGES

"I bargained with Life for a penny
    And Life would pay no more,
However I begged at evening,
    As I counted my scanty score.
For Life is just an employer,
    He gives you what you ask;
But once you have set the wages,
    Why you must bear the task.
I worked for a menial's hire,
    Only to learn, dismayed,
That any wage I had asked of Life,
    Life would have paid."

ANONYMOUS

SAY NOT THE STRUGGLE NOUGHT AVAILETH

Say not the struggle nought availeth,
    The labour and the wounds are vain,
The enemy faints not, nor faileth,
    And as things have been they remain.

If hopes were dupes, fears may be liars;
   It may be, in yon smoke conceal'd,
Your comrades chase e'en now the fliers,
   And, but for you, possess the field.

For while the tired waves, vainly breaking,
   Seem here no painful inch to gain,
Far back, through creeks and inlets making,
   Comes silent, flooding in, the main.

And not by eastern windows only,
   When daylight comes, comes in the light,
In front, the sun climbs slow, how slowly,
   But westward, look, the land is bright.

ARTHUR HUGH CLOUGH

EVERY YEAR

Life is a count of losses,
     Every year;
For the weak are heavier crosses,
     Every year;
Lost Springs with sobs replying
Unto weary Autumns' sighing,
While those we love are dying,
     Every year.

The days have less of gladness,
     Every year;
The nights more weight of sadness,
     Every year;
Fair Springs no longer charm us,
The wind and weather harm us,
The threats of death alarm us,
     Every year.

There come new cares and sorrows,
     Every year;
Dark days and darker morrows,
     Every year;

The ghosts of dead loves haunt us,
The ghosts of changed friends taunt us,
And disappointments daunt us,
  Every year.

To the Past go more dead faces,
  Every year;
As the loved leave vacant places,
  Every year;
Everywhere the sad eyes meet us,
In the evening's dusk they greet us,
And to come to them entreat us,
  Every year.

"You are growing old," they tell us,
  "Every year;
"You are more alone," they tell us,
  "Every year;
"You can win no new affection,
"You have only recollection,
"Deeper sorrow and dejection,
  Every year."

Too true! Life's shores are shifting,
  Every year;
And we are seaward drifting,
  Every year;
Old places, changing, fret us,
The living more forget us,
There are fewer to regret us,
  Every year.

But the truer life draws nigher,
  Every year;
And its Morning-star climbs higher,
  Every year;
Earth's hold on us grows slighter,
And the heavy burthen lighter,
And the Dawn Immortal brighter
  Every year.

ALBERT PIKE

OUR CABLETOW

Sometimes we hardly know its there,
  Our guiding cabletow;
If we go down the paths of right,
  Its hold we never know;
But if we start the way that's wrong,
It has a sudden way that's strong,
And makes us heed its strength to lead
  Down paths we ought to go.

And yet how good a thing to feel.
  How fine a thing to know,
That when the baser actions seek
  To wreck and overthrow,
When worldly appetites deprave,
Or lower passions would enslave,
We then can feel, like gripping steel,
  Our guiding cabletow.

GEORGE B. STAFF

GET AWAY FROM THE CROWD

Get away from the crowd for a while, and think. Stand on one side
and let the world run by, while you get acquainted with yourself and
see what kind of a fellow you are. Ask yourself hard questions about
yourself. Ascertain, from original sources, if you are really the manner
of man you say you are; and if you are always honest; if you always
tell the square, perfect truth in business details; if your life is as good
and upright at eleven o'clock at night as it is at noon; if you are as good
a temperance man on a fishing excursion as you are on a Sunday-
school picnic; if you are as good when you go to the city as you are
at home; if, in short, you are really the sort of man your father hopes
you are and your sweetheart believes you are. Get on intimate terms
with yourself, my boy, and, believe me, every time you come out of
one of those private interviews you will be a stronger, better, purer
man.

ROBERT BURDETTE

DON'T WORRY

Do not be troubled because you have not great virtues. God made a million spears of grass where He made one tree. The earth is fringed and carpeted not with forests but with grasses. Only have enough of little virtues and common fidelities and you need not mourn because you are neither a hero nor a saint.

HENRY WARD BEECHER

Prudence and Temperance

Prudence in Masonry means wisdom; wisdom was anciently a cardinal virtue and the mere changing of the syllables by which it is denominated does not change its nature. It is the wisdom which was meant by the writer of Proverbs, who said, "the heart of the prudent getteth knowledge."

Freemasonry is a system of wisdom of heart, wisdom of mind, wisdom, if the Mason so wills it, of soul. It is an approach of man to his Creator. It is a looking forward to better days and a looking up to higher things. Its whole structure is aimed at helping a man in the formation of good character. Wisdom is an essential for this, from thinking, rather than from education and teaching. Consider prudence as meaning a wisdom of both heart and mind and it becomes something high and holy and much more impressive than mere precaution, judged by the modern and colloquial meaning of the word prudence. . . . Therefore, a man is prudent when he allows wisdom to rule his actions.

CARL H. CLAUDY

Brethren do not encourage a craftsman to be conspicuous by his mysteries; do not encourage a craftsman to be conspicuous by his emblems; but always encourage a craftsman to be conspicuous by his devotion to the sublime principles of Freemasonry. Welcome the cultivation and practice of all the good and beautiful in our ritual, but avoid undue display before the world that Free and Accepted Masons are in possession of some great and unknown secrets of untold magnitude and importance.

JOHN W. VROOMAN

Thought will not work, except in silence; neither will virtue work, except in secrecy.

THOMAS CARLYLE

BE ON GUARD

Round the ancient Lodges,
  Men were set on guard,
North and south and east and west,
  Keeping watch and ward.
Silent, steady, sleepless,
  Keen of ear and eye—
On the pathway where they stood
  No one might creep by.

As the covenanters
  In each hidden glen
Kept a watch and ward without,
  Posted earnest men—
Not as shields of evil,
  Be it understood:
But they knew to keep the faith
  They must guard the good.

Near the ancient Lodges
  None might come to see;
None might come to listen there
  Save a sign gave he,
For the ancient Lodges,
  As those of today,
Kept the outer, creeping folk
  Very far away.

But, today, each Mason
  Has a duty high:
He must stand, a sentinel
  To all that come nigh;
He must guard Freemasonry,
  Must protect its name
As he would his gate or door
  Or a woman's name.

How, then, shall we do this?
Word and deed must bear
Evidence of what is in
  Compass, plumb and square!
So that they who watch us
  In the daily crowd
Shall proclaim that Masonry
  Is high, and clean, and proud!

WILBUR D. NESBIT

THE CABLE-TOW

There is not a man today who, having sought happiness outside of himself in material possessions or in fame or glory, is satisfied and happy within himself. True wisdom is to be gained within ourselves, by releasing ourselves from the things which bind us to ignorance and darkness and by cultivating the good, the pure, the beautiful and the true within ourselves.

From what must we release ourselves? From slavery to adverse and undesirable conditions, circumstances, habits, thoughts and environments.

How? by removing the Cable-Tow.

And what does the Cable-Tow stand for? Every strand of the cable-tow stands for some vice, weakness, habit, or shortcoming. . . . Freemasonry teaches no impractical lessons. Its formula consisting of rules and tenets for the guidance of the living of a successful life, has been tried and tested and lived by those who have gone before us, and it is for us to try them out in our lives and find them equally beneficial . . .

Thus, release yourself from the strand of laziness. It binds you to ignorance, failure and stagnation. Do not be lazy with yourself. Mental laziness is one of our worst enemies. We are too lazy to use our minds. We find it trouble to think for ourselves. Yet thought precedes action, and moulds our lives for failure or success. Dare to think for yourself, don't let others do it for you. Think only constructive, upbuilding, cheerful, optimistic thoughts.

Release yourself from anger and passion. Nothing is accomplished through anger. It weans away from you friends who otherwise would help you. It makes you and others miserable. Passion results in consuming your vitality which otherwise would go into productive channels. Passion wastes your energies, leaving you limp, weak and useless. We speak of the conservation of our natural resources. Let us apply conservation with ourselves. Let us conserve our forces, energies, potencies and capabilities for worthy and noble works.

Release yourself from self-indulgence. Indulgence in drink, in food and idle thinking leads to defeat and not success. The successful men, the men who are up and doing, do not indulge and pamper themselves, but endeavour to discipline themselves.

Release yourself from physical debility. No man can accomplish any good in this world while being handicapped by physical weakness. Strength of body and mind, virility, energy and manhood are absolutely essential to a successful life. Build up your body and mind. Try to control your mind. Let your thoughts not wander but master them and direct them in creative channels. Notice the successful men are full of power, energy and magnetism. They draw people to them, while the weak men repel people.

Release yourself from pride. More men remain in darkness and ignorance through false pride than through any other reason. Most men are too proud to own up they don't know, or that they are ignorant. And this pride prevents them from seeking the assistance of good men who could help them in knowledge and understanding. A wise man is meek and lowly and humble, while only fools are filled with pride. Some men prefer to remain in darkness rather than admit they are ignorant. Put pride aside, seek the company of good men who can help you.

Release yourself from worry. Worry never solved your problems. In fact, by worrying you weaken your mental powers so that you have less chance of solving your problems. Some say, "How can I stop worrying when adversity faces me?" Well, you have will power. Use it. Change your thought. Think of success. Think that you will come out on top. If you don't you will at least come out better than by worrying about your troubles.

These are some of the things you must release yourself from. As you study yourself you will find, oh, so many things from which you must become free.

Happiness and advancement in life go hand in hand; and if we are to possess them we must look within ourselves, in our make-up and discover the causes that hold us back. For, in most cases, the causes can be discovered within ourselves. Don't be an ostrich and hide your head in the sand and say there is nothing the matter with you. Don't be blind to your faults. Seek them out and eliminate them from your being.

A. W. WITT

TUBAL CAIN

Old Tubal Cain was a man of might,
　In the days when earth was young;
By the fierce red light of his furnace bright
　The strokes of his hammer rung;
And he lifted high his brawny hand
　On the iron glowing clear
Till the sparks rushed out in scarlet showers,
　As he fashioned the sword and spear;
And he sang, "Hurrah for my handiwork!
　Hurrah for the spear and sword!
Hurrah for the hand that shall wield these well,
　For he shall be king and lord!"

To Tubal Cain came many a one,
　As he wrought by his roaring fire,
And each one prayed for a strong steel blade,
　As the crown of his desire;
And he made them weapons sharp and strong,
　Till they shouted loud for glee,
And gave him gifts of pearl and gold,
　And spoils of the forest free;
And they sang, "Hurrah for Tubal Cain,
　Who hath given us strength anew!
Hurrah for the smith! Hurrah for the fire!
　And hurrah for the metal true!"

But a sudden change came o'er his heart,
　Ere the setting of the sun;
And Tubal Cain was filled with pain
　For the evil he had done.
He saw that men, with rage and hate,
　Made war upon their kind;
That the land was red with the blood they shed,
　In their lust for carnage blind;
And he said, "Alas! that ever I made,
　Or that skill of mine should plan
The spear and the sword, for men whose joy
　Is to slay their fellow man!"

And for many a day old Tubal Cain
  Sat brooding o'er his woe,
And his hand forebore to smite the ore,
  And his furnace smouldered low.
But he rose at last with a cheerful face
  And a bright, courageous eye,
And bared his strong arm for work,
  While the quick flames mounted high,
And he sang, "Hurrah for my handiwork!"
  And the red sparks lit the air;
"Not alone for the blade was the bright steel made."
  And he fashioned the first ploughshare,

And the men taught wisdom from the past,
  In friendship joined their hands,
Hung the sword in the hall, the spear on the wall,
  And ploughed the willing lands.
And sang, "Hurrah for Tubal Cain!
  Our staunch good friend is he;
And for the ploughshare and the plough,
  To him our praise shall be;
But while oppression lifts its head,
  Or a tyrant would be lord,
Though we may thank him for the plough,
  We'll not forget the sword!"

CHARLES MACKAY

Ambition, avarice, personal animosity, party opposition, and many
other motives, not more laudable than these, are apt to operate as
well upon those who support, as upon those who oppose, the right side
of a question. Were there not even these inducements to moderation,
nothing could be more ill-judged than that intolerant spirit, which has,
at all times, characterized political parties. For, in politics as in religion,
it is equally absurd to aim at making proselytes by fire and sword.
Heresies in either can rarely be cured by persecution.

ALEXANDER HAMILTON

Everything that takes place is a symbol. In representing itself perfectly it suggests what lies beyond. In this reflection extreme modesty and extreme pretentiousness seem to me combined.

JOHANN WOLFGANG VON GOETHE

I daily examine myself in a threefold manner: in my transactions with men, if I am upright; in my intercourse with friends, if I am faithful; and whether I illustrate the teachings of my master in my conduct.

CONFUCIUS

Learn, then, what MORALS Critics ought to show,
For 'tis but half a Judge's task to know.
'Tis not enough, taste, judgment, learning join;
In all you speak, let truth and candour shine:
That not alone what to your sense is due
All may allow; but seek your friendship too.
  Be silent always, when you doubt your sense;
And speak, tho' sure, with seeming diffidence:
Some positive, persisting fops we know,
Who, if once wrong, will needs be always so;
But you, with pleasure own your errors past,
And make each day a Critique on the last.
  'Tis not enough your counsel still be true;
Blunt truths more mischief than nice falsehoods do;
Men must be taught as if you taught them not,
And things unknown propos'd as things forgot.
Without Good-Breeding, truth is disapprov'd;
That only makes superior sense belov'd.
  Be niggards of advice on no pretence;
For the worst avarice is that of sense.
With mean complaisance ne'er betray your trust,
Nor be so civil as to prove unjust.
Fear not the anger of the wise to raise;
Those best can bear reproof, who merit praise.

ALEXANDER POPE

Temperance as a virtue applying to only strong drink is modern; temperance as a virtue set forth in the Old Testament meant a reasonable restraint upon *all* desires; excess was deplorable in those days whether it was food, or drink, or lust, or war, or revenge, or pride, or covetousness, or sloth, or malice, or indifference to others and so on. In the Masonic teaching of temperance means, literally a tempering— Latin *temporare*, to apportion, moderate, regulate all human actions; in this it is akin to the ancient wisdom which makes it one of the four cardinal virtues.

CARL H. CLAUDY

The last observation that I shall now mention of the Cardinal de Retz is, "That a secret is more easily kept by a good many people, than one commonly imagines." By this he meant a secret of importance, among people interested in the keeping of it. And it is certain that people of business know the importance of secrecy, and will observe it, where they are concerned in the event. To go and tell any friend, wife, or mistress, any secret with which they have nothing to do, is discovering to them such an unretentive weakness, as must convince them that you will tell it to twenty others, and consequently that they may reveal it without the risk of being discovered. But a secret properly communicated only to those who are to be concerned in the thing in question, will probably be kept by them though they should be a good many. Little secrets are commonly told again, but great ones are generally kept.

LORD CHESTERFIELD

Search with the greatest care, into the character of those whom you converse with; endeavour to discover their predominate passions, their prevailing weaknesses, their vanities, their follies, and their humours, with all the right and wrong, wise and silly springs of human actions, which make such inconsistent and whimsical beings of us rational creatures. A moderate share of penetration, with great attention, will infallibly make these necessary discoveries. This is the true knowledge of the world; and the world is a country which nobody ever yet knew by description; one must travel through it one's self to be acquainted with it. . . . Human nature is the same all over the world; but its operations are so varied by education and habit, that one must see it in all its dresses in order to be intimately acquainted with it. . . . Civility, which is a disposition to accommodate and oblige others, is essentially the same in every country; but good-breeding, as it is called, which is the manner of exerting that disposition, is different in almost every country, and merely local; and every man of sense imitates and conforms to that local good-breeding of the place which he is at. A conformity and flexibility of manners is necessary in the course of the world; that is, with regard to all things which are not wrong in themselves. The *versatile ingenium* is the most useful of all. It can turn itself from one object to another, assuming the proper manner for each. It can be serious with the grave, cheerful with the gay, and trifling with the frivolous. Endeavour by all means, to acquire this talent, for it is a very great one.

LORD CHESTERFIELD

The moral man conforms himself to his life circumstances; he does not desire anything outside of his position. Finding himself in a position of wealth and honour, he lives as becomes one living in a position of wealth and honour. Finding himself in a position of poverty and humble circumstances, he lives as becomes one living in a position of poverty and humble circumstances. Finding himself in uncivilized countries, he lives as becomes one living in uncivilized countries.

Finding himself in circumstances of danger and difficulty, he acts according to what is required of a man under such circumstances.

In one word, the moral man can find himself in no situation in life in which he is not master of himself.

In a high position he does not domineer over his subordinates. In a subordinate position he does not court the favours of his superiors. He puts in order his own personal conduct and seeks nothing from others; hence he has no complaint to make. He complains not against God nor rails against man.

Thus it is that the moral man lives out the even tenor of his life, calmly waiting for the appointment of God, whereas the vulgar person takes to dangerous courses, expecting the uncertain chances of luck.

In the practice of archery we have something resembling the principle in a moral man's life. When the archer misses the centre of the target, he turns round and seeks for the cause of his failure within himself.

CONFUCIUS

MEN ARE FOUR

He who knows not, and
Knows not he knows not—
He is a fool—shun him.

He who knows not, and
Knows he knows not—
He is a child—trust him.

He who knows, and
Knows not he knows—
He is asleep—wake him.

He who knows, and
Knows he knows—
He is wise—follow him.

ARABIAN PROVERB

GEORGE WASHINGTON

Perhaps the strongest feature in his character was prudence, never
acting until every circumstance, every consideration was maturely
weighed . . . His integrity was most pure, his justice the most inflexible
I have ever known, no motives of interest or consanguinity, of friendship or hatred, being able to bias his decision. He was, indeed, in every
sense of the words, a wise, a good, and a great man. His temper was
naturally irritable and high toned; but reflection and resolution had
obtained a firm and habitual ascendency over it. If, however, it broke
its bonds, he was most tremendous in his wrath.

In his expenses he was honourable, but exact; liberal in contributions
to whatever promised utility; but frowning and unyielding on all
visionary projects and all unworthy calls on his charity. His heart was
not warm in its affections; but he exactly calculated every man's value,
and gave him a solid esteem proportioned to it . . .

Although in the circle of friends, where he might be unreserved with safety, he took a free share in conversation, his colloquial talents were not above mediocrity, possessing neither copiousness of ideas, nor fluency of words. In public, when called on for a sudden opinion, he was unready, short and embarrassed. Yet he wrote readily, rather diffusely, in an easy and correct style . . . .

On the whole, his character was, in its mass, perfect, in nothing bad, in a few points indifferent; and it may be truly said, that never did nature and fortune combine more perfectly to make a man great, and to place him . . . . in an everlasting remembrance.

THOMAS JEFFERSON

Silence and Secrecy! Altars might still be raised to them (were this an altar building time) for universal worship. Silence is the element in which great things fashion themselves together; that at length they may emerge, full-formed and majestic, into the daylight of Life, which they are henceforth to rule. Not William the Silent only, but all the considerable men I have known, and the most undiplomatic and unstrategic of these, forbore to babble of what they were creating and projecting. Nay, in thy own mean perplexities, do thou thyself but hold thy tongue for one day; on the morrow, how much clearer are thy purposes and duties; what wreck and rubbish have those mute workmen within thee swept away, when intrusive noises were shut out! Speech is too often not, as the Frenchman defined it, the art of concealing Thought; but of quite stifling and suspending Thought, so that there is none to conceal. Speech too is great, but not the greatest. As the Swiss inscription says, "Speech is silvern, Silence is golden;" or as I might rather express it: Speech is of Time, Silence is of Eternity.

Bees will not work except in darkness; Thought will not work except in Silence: neither will virtue work except in Secrecy. Let not thy left hand know what thy right hand doeth! Neither shalt thou prate even to thy own heart of "those secrets known to all." Is not Shame the soil of all Virtue, of all good manners and good morals? Like other plants, Virtue will not grow unless its root be hidden, buried from the eyes of the sun. Let the sun shine on it, nay do but look at it privily thyself, the root withers, and no flower will gladden thee.

THOMAS CARLYLE

Of kin to the so incalcuble influences of Concealment, and connected with still greater things, is the wondrous agency of Symbols. In a Symbol there is concealment and yet revelation; here, therefore, by Silence and Speech acting together, comes a double significance. And if both the Speech be itself high, and the Silence fit and noble, how expressive will their union be! Thus is many a painted Device, a simple Seal-emblem, the commonest Truth stands out to us proclaimed with quite new emphasis.

THOMAS CARLYLE

> Avoid Extremes; and shun the fault of such
> Who still are pleas'd too little or too much.
> At ev'ry trifle scorn to take offence:
> That always shows great pride, or little sense;
> Those heads, as stomachs, are not sure the best
> Which nauseate all, and nothing can digest.
> Yet let not each gay Turn thy rapture move,
> For fools admire, but men of sense approve:
> As things seem large which we through mists descry,
> Dulness is ever apt to magnify.

ALEXANDER POPE

... It is always the part of prudence to face every claimant and pay every just demand on your time, your talents, or your heart. Always pay; for first or last you must pay your entire debt.

RALPH WALDO EMERSON

Every excellency, and every virtue, has its kindred vice or weakness; and if carried beyond certain bounds, sinks into one or the other. Generosity often runs into profusion, economy into avarice, courage into rashness, caution into timidity, and so on:— insomuch that, I believe, there is more judgment required, for the proper conduct of our virtues, than for avoiding their opposite vices. Vice, in its true light, is so deformed, that it shocks us at first sight, and would hardly ever seduce us, if it did not, at first, wear the mask of some virtue. But virtue is, in itself, so beautiful, that it charms us at first sight; engages us more and more upon further acquaintance; and, as with other beauties, we think excess impossible; it is here that judgment is necessary, to moderate and direct the effects of an excellent cause.

LORD CHESTERFIELD

A real man of fashion and pleasures observes decency; at least neither borrows nor affects vices; and if he unfortunately has any, he gratifies them with choice, delicacy, and secrecy.

I have not mentioned the pleasures of the mind (which are the solid and permanent ones), because they do not come under the head of what people commonly call pleasures; which they seem to confine to the senses. The pleasure of virtue, of charity, and of learning is true and lasting pleasure; with which I hope you will be well and long acquainted.

LORD CHESTERFIELD

Many young people adopt pleasures, for which they have not the least taste, only because they are called by that name. They often mistake so totally, as to imagine that debauchery is pleasure. You must allow that drunkenness, which is equally destructive to body and mind, is a fine pleasure. Gaming, that draws you into a thousand scrapes, leaves you penniless, and gives you the air and manners of an outrageous madman, is another most exquisite pleasure; is it not? As to running after women, the consequences of that vice are only the loss of one's nose, the total destruction of health, and, not unfrequently, the being run through the body.

These, you see, are all trifles; yet this is the catalogue of pleasures of most of those young people, who never reflecting themselves, adopt, indiscriminately, what others choose to call by the seducing name of pleasure. I am thoroughly persuaded you will not fall into such errors; and that, in the choice of your amusements, you will be directed by reason, and a discerning taste. The true pleasures of a gentleman are those of the table, but within the bound of moderation; good company, that is to say, people of merit; moderate play, which amuses, without any interested views; and sprightly gallant conversations with women of fashion and sense.

These are the real pleasures of a gentleman; which occasion neither sickness, shame, nor repentence. Whatever exceeds them, becomes low vice, brutal passion, debauchery, and insanity of mind; all of which, far from giving satisfaction, bring on dishonour and disgrace.

LORD CHESTERFIELD

Friendship

Masonry is Friendship—friendship, first, with the Great Companion, of whom our own hearts tell us, who is always nearer to us than we are to ourselves, and whose inspiration and help is the greatest fact of human experience. To be in harmony with His purposes, to be open to His suggestions, to be conscious of fellowship with Him—that is Masonry on its Godward side. Then, turning manward, friendship sums it all up. To be friends with all men, however they may differ from us in creed, colour, or condition; to fill every human relation with the spirit of friendship; is there anything more or better than this that the wisest and best of men can hope to do? Such is the spirit of Masonry; such is its ideal, and if to realize it all at once is denied us, surely it means much to see it, love it, and labour to make it come true.

Nor is this Spirit of Friendship a mere sentiment held by a sympathetic, and therefore unstable, fraternity, which would dissolve the concrete features of humanity into a vague blur of misty emotion. No; it has its roots in a profound philosophy which sees that the universe is friendly, and that men must learn to be friends if they would live as befits the world in which they live, as well as their own origin and destiny. For, since God is the life of all that was, is, and is to be; and since we are all born into the world by one high wisdom and one vast love, we are brothers to the last man of us, forever! For better for worse, for richer for poorer, in sickness and in health, and even after death us do part, all men are held together by ties of spiritual kindship, sons of one eternal Friend. Upon this fact human fraternity rests, and it is the basis of the plea of Masonry, not only for freedom, but for friendship among men.

JOSEPH FORT NEWTON

A BROTHER'S HAND

When you're feeling all downhearted,
And life's hard to understand,
Say, it's fine to feel the pressure
Of a Brother's friendly hand.

Just to know he sympathizes,
   Though he doesn't say a word;
How it start's your courage climbing,
   As your heart is touched and stirred.

With an arm across your shoulders,
   And a grip you love to find,
How it makes you feel the bounding
   Of the hearts of humankind.

It is just a little token
   Of an ever growing band,
For there's faith and hope and courage
   In a Brother's friendly hand!

GEORGE B. STAFF

"WE ARE TWO BROTHERS"

Give me your hand:
You are rich; I am poor:
Your wealth is your power, and by it you tread
A wide open path: where for me is a door
That is locked: and before it are worry and dread.
We are sundered, are we,
As two men can be
But we are two brothers in Freemasonry
So give me your hand.

Give me your hand:
You are great: I'm unknown:
You travel abroad with a permanent fame;
I go on a way unlauded, alone,
With hardly a man to hear of my name:
We are sundered, are we,
As two men can be,
But we are two brothers in Freemasonry
So give me your hand.

Give me your hand:
You are old; I am young;
The years in your heart their wisdom have sown;
But knowledge speaks not by my faltering tongue,
And small is the wisdom I claim as my own:
We are sundered, are we,
As two men can be,
But we are two brothers in Freemasonry
So give me your hand.

H. L. HAYWOOD

TWO AT A FIRESIDE

I built a chimney for a comrade old,
    I did the service not for hope or hire—
And then I travelled on in winter's cold,
    Yet all the day I glowed before the fire.

EDWIN MARKHAM

NEW FRIENDS AND OLD FRIENDS

Make new friends, but keep the old;
Those are silver, these are gold.
New-made friendships, like new wine,
Age will mellow and refine.
Friendships that have stood the test—
Time and change—are surely best;
Brow may wrinkle, hair grow grey;
Friendship never knows decay.
For 'mid old friends, tried and true,
Once more we our youth renew.
But old friends, alas! may die;
New friends must their place supply.
Cherish friendship in your breast—
New is good, but old is best;
Make new friends, but keep the old;
Those are silver, these are gold.

JOSEPH PARRY

Sentiments are what unites people, opinions what separates them. Sentiments are a simple bond that gathers us together; opinions represent the principle of variety that scatters. The friendships of youth are founded on the former, the cliques of old age are to be blamed on the latter. If we could only realize this early and arrive at a liberal view as regards others in cultivating our own attitude of mind, we would be more conciliatory and try to collect the bond of sentiment that opinion has dispersed.

JOHANN WOLFGANG VON GOETHE

PRAYER

Anything, God, but hate;
I have known it in my day,
And the best it does is scar your soul
And eat your heart away.
Man must know more than hate,
As the years go rolling on;
For the stars survive and the spring survives,
Only man denies the dawn.
God, if I have but one prayer
Before the cloud-wrapped end,
I'm sick of hate and the waste it makes.
Let me be my brother's friend.

ANONYMOUS

MY CREED

I would be true, for there are those who trust me;
I would be pure, for there are those who care;
I would be strong, for there is much to suffer;
I would be brave, for there is much to dare.

I would be friend of all—the foe, the friendless;
I would be giving and forget the gift;
I would be humble, for I know my weakness;
I would look up—and laugh—and love—and lift.

HOWARD ARNOLD WALTER

One may deal with things without love; one may cut down trees, make bricks, hammer iron without love; but you cannot deal with me without it, just as one cannot deal with bees without being careful. If you deal carelessly with bees you will injure them, and will yourself be injured. And so with men. It cannot be otherwise, because natural love is the fundamental law of human life. It is true that a man cannot force another to love him, as he can force him to work for him; but it does not follow that a man may deal with men without love, especially to demand anything from them. If you feel no love, sit still, occupy yourself with things, with yourself, only not with men.

LEO TOLSTOY

JUST FRIENDS

'Twould never do for God to live across the street,
Or in the house next door, where we should daily meet;
So in His wisdom and His love he sometimes sends
His angels kind to walk with us—we call them "friends."

Just friends—one word! But letters can express
A wealth of sympathy and pure unselfishness.
One syllable—a single breath can form it—friends,
Yet O how much our happiness on them depends!

When trouble comes, or loss, when grief is ours to bear,
They come, our friends, with words of cheer, our load to share.
How could we face defeat without a friend's caress?
Had we no friend to praise, how bare would be success!

A friend will never doubt, though foes may villify,
Nor is there need, with him, the falsehood to deny,
And should we go astray or guilt our fair fame kill,
Though conscious of our faults, forgive and love us still.

'Tis not God's plan that we shall see Him face to face,
Yet He would hedge us in with His abounding grace;
And so His messengers of love to earth He sends.
They're angels, but we know it not, and call them "friends."

GEORGE H. FREE

THE FRIEND WHO JUST STANDS BY

When trouble comes your soul to try,
You love the friend who just "stands by."
Perhaps there's nothing he can do—
The thing is strictly up to you;
For there are troubles all your own,
And paths the soul must tread alone;
Times when love cannot smooth the road
Nor friendship lift the heavy load,
But just to know you have a friend
Who will "stand by" until the end,
Whose sympathy through all endures,
Whose warm handclasp is always yours—
It helps, someway, to pull you through,
Although there's nothing he can do.
And so with fervent heart you cry,
"God bless the friend who just 'stands by.' "

B. Y. WILLIAMS

THE ARROW AND THE SONG

I shot an arrow into the air,
It fell to earth, I knew not where;
For, so swiftly it flew, the sight
Could not follow it in its flight.

I breathed a song into the air,
It fell to earth, I knew not where;
For who has sight so keen and strong
That it can follow the flight of song?

Long, long afterward, in an oak
I found the arrow, still unbroke;
And the song, from beginning to end,
I found again in the heart of a friend.

HENRY WADSWORTH LONGFELLOW

FRIENDSHIP

Oh, the comfort—the inexpressible comfort of feeling safe with
   a person,
Having neither to weigh thoughts,
Nor measure words—but pouring them
All right out—just as they are—
Chaff and grain together—
Certain that a faithful hand will
Take and sift them—
Keep what is worth keeping—
And with the breath of kindness
Blow the rest away.

DINAH MARIA MULOCK CRAIK

FIDELITY

Desert not your friend in danger or distress. Too many there are in
the world whose attachment to those they call friends is confined to
the day of their prosperity. As long as that continues, they are, or
appear to be, affectionate and cordial. But as their friend is under a
cloud, they begin to withdraw and separate their interests from his.
In friendship of this sort, the heart assuredly has never had much concern. For the great test of true friendship is, constancy in the hour of
danger—adherence in the season of distress. When your friend is
calumniated, then is the time openly and boldly to espouse his cause.
When his situation is changed, or misfortunes are fast gathering around
him, then is the time of affording prompt and zealous aid. When sickness or infirmity occasions him to be neglected by others, that is the
opportunity which every real friend will seize of redoubling all the
affectionate attention which love suggests. These are the important
duties, the sacred claims of friendship, which religion and virtue enforce on every worthy mind. To show yourselves warm in this
manner in the cause of your friend, commands esteem, even in those
who have personal interests in opposing him. This honourable zeal of
friendship has, in every age, attracted the veneration of mankind. It
has consecrated to the latest posterity the names of those who have
given up their fortunes and have exposed their lives on behalf of the

friends whom they loved; while ignominy and disgrace have ever been the portion of those who deserted their friends in the hour of distress.

ANONYMOUS

OUTWITTED

He drew a circle that shut me out—
Heretic, rebel, a thing to flout.
But Love and I had the wit to win:
We drew a circle that took him in!

EDWIN MARKHAM

WARMTH AND WELCOME

Across the crowd-thronged city ways
When night hangs black and friendless there,
A tide of strangers ebbs and plays
Along each cheerless thoroughfare,
And never a face lights up to see
One's self to pass, and none to care
How lone and weary one may be.

'Tis then unto one's Lodge one turns
For there he finds within the door
The fire of hearty welcome burns:
If one's not known its flames the more
Send forth a warmth his breast to fill
Until he finds his joy returns
Within that haven of good will.

The Mason's secret lies in this,—
"A stranger here, ye took me in";
Its Royal Art would stray amiss
Amid the world's harsh hue and din
If warmth and welcome were to die;
Its greatest strength in these consists;
Of these is made its Mystic Tie.

H. L. HAYWOOD

219

GOOD FELLOWSHIP

Ho, brother, it's the handclasp and the good word and the smile
That does the most and helps the most to make the world worth
     while!
It's all of us together, or it's only you and I—
A ringing song of friendship, and the heart beats high;
A ringing song of friendship, and a word or two of cheer!
Then all the world is gladder and the bending sky is clear!

It's you and I together—and we're brothers one and all
When even through good fellowship we hear the subtle call,
Whenever in the ruck of things we feel the helping hand
Or see the deeper glow that none but we may understand—
Then all the world is good to us and all is worth the while;
Ho, brother, it's the handclasp and the good word and the smile!

WILBUR D. NESBIT

As you get older and your world keeps shrinking, you sometimes
think with amazement of the times when you trifled away friendships—insensitive in the reckless folly of youth to the wounds you
inflicted and indifferent to healing them.

JOHANN WOLFGANG VON GOETHE

TO A FRIEND

He was my friend. His presence was to me
Like perfume from a cherry-blossom tree,
His voice brought calm,—it soothed like tuneful chimes
A-playing slowly, sacred peaceful rhymes.

He was my friend. His handclasp steadied me.
His grasp drew me there where I longed to be.
His thoughts entwined with mine in rendezvous
Like mated stars in yonder peaceful blue.

He was my friend, a friend worth more than gold,
More than the stores of fabled Croesus hold.
He brought me faith, contentment, hope and cheer.
When he was here, then too, God's love was near.

WALTER H. BONN

FAREWELL TO THE BRETHREN

(This poem was written by Burns when because of financial difficulties he had
decided to accept a post in Jamaica. Fortunately this plan was never carried out.)

Adieu! a heart-warm, fond adieu!
Dear Brothers of the Mystic tie!
Ye favoured, ye enlighten'd few,
Companions of my social joy!
Tho' I to foreign lands must hie,
Pursuing Fortune's slidd'ry ba',
With melting heart, and brimful eye,
I'll mind you still, tho' far awa'.

Oft have I met your social band
And spent the cheerful, festive night:
Oft honoured with supreme command,
Presided o'er the Sons of Light;
And by the Hieroglyphic Bright,
Which none but Craftsmen ever saw!
Strong Mem'ry on my heart shall write
Those happy scenes, when far awa'.

May Freedom, Harmony, and Love,
Unite you in the Grand Design,
Beneath th' Omniscient Eye above—
The glorious Architect Divine—
That you keep th' Unerring Line,
Still rising by the Plummet's Law,
Till ORDER bright completely shine,
Shall be my pray'r when far awa'.

And you FAREWELL! whose merits claim
Justly the Highest Badge to wear!
Heav'n bless your honour'd noble NAME
To Masonry and Scotia dear.
At last request permit me here,
When yearly ye assemble a',
One round, I ask it with a tear
To him, the Bard that's far awa'.

ROBERT BURNS

AN ANCIENT MASONIC SONG

'Tis Masonry unites mankind,
    To gen'rous actions, forms the Soul;
In friendly Converse all conjoined,
    One Spirit animates the whole.

Where'er aspiring Domes arise,
    Wherever sacred Altars stand;
These Altars blaze into the skies,
    The Domes proclaim the Mason's Hand.

As passions rough the Soul disguise,
    Till Science cultivates the Mind;
So the rude Stone unshapen lies,
    Till by the Mason's art refin'd.

Tho' still our chief Concern and Care
    Be to deserve the Brother's Name:
Yet ever mindful of the Fair,
    Their kindest Influence we claim.

Let wretches at our Manhood rail;
    But they who once our Order prove,
Will own that we who build so well,
    With equal energy can love.

ANONYMOUS

Be courteous to all, but intimate with few; and let those few be well tried before you give them your confidence. True friendship is a plant of slow growth, and must undergo and withstand the shocks of adversity before it is entitled to the apellation. Let your heart feel for the afflictions and distresses of every one, and let your hand give in proportion to your purse; remembering always the estimation of the widow's mite, that it is not every one that asketh that deserveth charity; all, however, are worthy of the inquiry, or the deserving may suffer.

Do not conceive that fine clothes make fine men, any more than fine feathers make fine birds. A plain, genteel dress is more admired, obtains more credit, than lace and embroidery, in the eyes of the judicious and sensible.

GEORGE WASHINGTON

I SAT IN LODGE WITH YOU

There is a saying filled with cheer,
  Which calls a man to fellowship.
It means as much for him to hear
  As lies within the brother-grip.
Nay, more! It opens wide the way
  To friendliness sincere and true;
There are no strangers when you say
  To me: "I sat in lodge with you."

When that is said, then I am known;
  There is no questioning nor doubt;
I need not walk my path alone
  Nor from my fellows be shut out.
Those words hold all of brotherhood
  And help me face the world anew—
There's something deep and rich and good
  In this: "I sat in lodge with you."

223

Though in far lands one needs must roam,
By sea and shore and hill and plain,
Those words bring him a touch of home
And lighten tasks that seem in vain.
Men's faces are no longer strange
But seem as those he always knew
When some one brings the joyous change
With his: "I sat in lodge with you."

So you, my brother, now and then
Have often put me in your debt
By showing forth to other men
That you your friends do not forget.
When all the world seems grey and cold
And I am weary, worn and blue,
Then comes this golden thought I hold—
You said: "I sat in lodge with you."

When to the last great Lodge you fare
My prayer is that I may be
One of your friends who wait you there,
Intent your smiling face to see.
We, with the warder at the gate,
Will have a pleasant task to do;
We'll call, though you come soon or late:
"Come in! We sat in lodge with you!"

WILBUR D. NESBIT

A faithful friend is a strong defense: and he that hath found him hath found a treasure.

Nothing can be compared to a faithful friend: and no weight of gold and silver is able to countervail the goodness of his fidelity.

A faithful friend is the medicine of life and immortality: and they that fear the Lord shall find him.

He that feareth God shall likewise have good friendship: because according to him shall his friend be.

ECCLESIASTICUS 6:14-17

(*Douay translation*)

WHAT CAME WE HERE TO DO?

Foot to foot, no matter where,
   Though far beyond my destined road,
If Brother needs a Brother's care,
   On foot I'll go and share his load.

Knee to knee, no selfish prayer
   Shall ever from my lips ascend,
For all who act upon the square,
   At least, henceforth, my knee shall bend.

Breast to breast, and this I swear,
   A Brother's secrets here shall sleep,
If told to me upon the square,
   Save those I am not bound to keep.

Hand to back, Oh, type of love!
   Fit emblem to adorn the skies,
Be this our task below, above,
   To help poor failing mortals rise.

Cheek to cheek, or mouth to ear,
   "We all like sheep have gone astray,"
May we good counsel give and bear
   'Til each shall find the better way.

J. M. JENKINS

I have often thought, that as longevity is generally desired, and I believe, generally expected, it would be wise to be continually adding to the number of our friends, that the loss of some may be supplied by others. Friendship, "the wine of life," should, like a well-stocked cellar, be thus continually renewed; and it is consolatory to think, that although we can seldom add what will equal the generous first *growths* of our youth, yet friendship becomes insensibly old in much less time than is commonly imagined, and not many years are required to make it very mellow and pleasant.

JAMES BOSWELL

HIGH RESOLVE

I'll hold my candle high, and then,
Perhaps, I'll see the hearts of men
Above the sordidness of life—
Beyond misunderstandings, strife,
Though many deeds that others do
Seem foolishness, and sinful, too,
Were I to take another's place,
I could not fill it with such grace.
And who am I to criticize
What I perceive with my dull eyes?
I'll hold my candle high, and then,
Perhaps, I'll see the hearts of men.

ANONYMOUS

Love of Home

In primitive society there were four institutions, equally Divine, equally sacred, all tokens of the solidarity of aspiration and obligation, of need and destiny, which binds humanity together. There was, first of all, and most fundamental, the Home—the corner stone of society and civilization, which satisfies more human needs than any other fellowship. It was crude, as all things were in the morning of time, yet it had in it the prophecy of that enshrinement of beauty and tenderness into which we were born, the memory of which hallows us still. The basic fact in the human story is the family as the unit of values, marking the life of man off from anything known or looked for in the animal world. To contrast its early simplicity with the religious and social refinement of today is to fill the word Progress with an unimagined meaning.

JOSEPH FORT NEWTON

GOD IN THE HOME

Anyone can build an altar; it requires a God to provide the flame. *Anybody can build a house; we need the Lord for the creation of a home.* A house is an agglomeration of brick and stones, with an assorted collection of manufactured goods; a home is the abiding-place of ardent affection, of fervent hope, of genial trust. There is many a homeless man who lives in a richly furnished house. There is many a fifteen-pound house in the crowded street which is an illuminated and beautiful home. The sumptuously furnished house may only be an exquisitely sculptured tomb; the scantily furnished house may be the very hearthstone of the eternal God. ... The New Testament does not say very much about homes; it says a great deal about the things that make them. It speaks about life and love and joy and peace and rest! If we get a house and put these into it, we shall have secured a home.

JOHN HENRY JOWETT

HOME

It takes a heap o'livin' in a house t' make it home,
A heap o'sun an' shadder, and ye sometimes have t'roam
Afore ye really 'preciate the things ye lef' behind,
An' hunger fer'em somehow, with'em allus on yer mind.
It don't make any differunce how rich ye get t'be,
How much yer chairs an' tables cost, how great yer luxury;
It ain't home t'ye though it be the palace of a king,
Until somehow yer soul is sort o'wrapped round everything.

Home ain't a place that gold can buy or get up in a minute;
Afore it's home there's got t' be a heap o'livin' in it;
Within the walls there's got t' be some babies born, and then
Right there ye've got t' bring 'em up t' women good, an' men;
And gradjerly, as time goes on, ye find ye wouldn't part
With anything they ever used—they've grown into yer heart:
The old high chairs, the playthings, too, the little shoes they wore
Ye hoard; an' if ye could ye'd keep the thumb-marks on the door.

Ye've got t'weep t' make it home, ye've got t' sit an' sigh
An' watch beside a loved one's bed, an' know that Death is nigh;
An' in the stillness o' the night t' see Death's angel come,
An' close the eyes o' her that smiled, an' leave her sweet voice
    dumb.
For these are scenes that grip the heart, an' when yer tears are
    dried,
Ye find the home is dearer than it was, an' sanctified;
An' tuggin' at ye always are the pleasant memories
O'her that was an' is no more—ye can't escape from these.

Ye've got to sing and dance fer years, ye've got t' romp an' play,
An' learn t' love the things ye have by usin' 'em each day;
Even the roses round the porch must blossom year by year
Afore they 'come a part o'ye, suggestin' someone dear
Who used t' love 'em long ago, and trained 'em just t' run
The way they do, so's they would get the early mornin' sun;
Ye've got to love each brick an' stone from cellar up t' dome:
It takes a heap o'livin' in a house to make it home.

EDGAR A. GUEST

A PRAYER FOR A LITTLE HOME

God send us a little home,
To come back to, when we roam.

Low walls and fluted tiles,
Wide windows, a view for miles.

Red firelight and deep chairs,
Small white beds upstairs—

Great talk in little nooks,
Dim colours, rows of books.

One picture on each wall,
Not many things at all.

God send us a little ground,
Tall trees stand round.

Homely flowers in brown sod,
Overhead, thy stars, O God.

God bless thee, when winds blow,
Our home, and all we know.

FLORENCE BONE

THE SOUL OF A HOUSE

The walls of a house are not built of wood, brick or stone, but of truth and loyalty.

Unpleasant sounds, the friction of living, the clash of personalities, are not deadened by Persian rugs or polished floors, but by conciliation, concession and self-control. . . .

The house is not a structure where bodies meet, but a hearthstone upon which flames mingle, separate flames of souls, which, the more perfectly they unite, the more clearly they shine and the straighter they rise toward heaven.

Your house is your fortress in a warring world, where a woman's hand buckles on your armour in the morning and soothes your fatigue and wounds at night.

The beauty of a house is harmony.

The security of a house is loyalty.

The joy of a house is love.

The plenty of a house is in children.

The rule of a house is service.

The comfort of a house is in contented spirits.

The maker of a house, of a real human house, is God himself, the same who made the stars and built the world.

FRANK CRANE

HOME IS WHERE THERE IS ONE TO LOVE US

Home's not merely four square walls,
Though with pictures hung and gilded;
Home is where Affection calls—
Filled with shrines the Hearth had builded!
Home! Go watch the faithful dove,
Sailing 'neath the heaven above us.
Home is where there's one to love!
Home is where there's one to love us.

Home's not merely roof and room,
It needs something to endear it;
Home is where the heart can bloom,
Where there's some kind lip to cheer it!
What is home with none to meet,
None to welcome, none to greet us?
Home is sweet, and only sweet,
Where there's one we love to meet us!

CHARLES SWAIN

PRAYER FOR FAMILY BLESSING

Lord, behold our family here assembled. We thank Thee for this place in which we dwell; for the love that unites us; for the peace accorded us this day; for the hope with which we expect the morrow; for the health, the work, the food, and the bright skies, that make our lives delightful; for our friends in all parts of the earth, and our friendly helpers in this foreign isle. Let peace abound in our small company. Purge out of every heart the lurking grudge. Give us grace and strength to forebear and to persevere. Offenders, give us the grace to accept and to forgive offenders. Forgetful ourselves, help us to bear cheerfully the forgetfulness of others. Give us courage and gaiety and the quiet mind. Spare us to our friends, soften to us our enemies. Bless us, if it may be, in all our innocent endeavours. If it may not, give us the strength to encounter that which is to come, that we may be brave in peril, constant in tribulation, temperate in wrath, and in all changes of fortune down to gates of death, loyal and loving one to another. As the clay to the potter, as the windmill to the wind, as children of their sire, we beseech of Thee the help and mercy, for Christ's sake.

ROBERT LOUIS STEVENSON

HOME, SWEET HOME

'Mid pleasures and palaces though we may roam,
Be it ever so humble, there's no place like home;
A charm from the sky seems to hallow us there,
Which, seek through the world, is ne'er met with elsewhere.
    Home, home, sweet, sweet home!
There's no place like home, oh, there's no place like home!

An exile from home, splendour dazzles in vain;
Oh, give me my lowly thatched cottage again!
The birds singing gayly, that came at my call—
Give me them—and the peace of mind, dearer than all!
    Home, home, sweet, sweet home!
There's no place like home, oh, there's no place like home!

I gaze on the moon as I tread the drear wild,
And feel that my mother now thinks of her child,
As she looks on that moon from our own cottage door
Thro' the woodbine, whose fragrance shall cheer me no more.
    Home, home, sweet, sweet home!
There's no place like home, oh, there's no place like home!

How sweet 'tis to sit 'neath a fond father's smile,
And the caress of a mother to soothe and beguile!
Let others delight 'mid new pleasure to roam,
But give me, oh, give me, the pleasures of home,
    Home, home, sweet, sweet home!
There's no place like home, oh, there's no place like home!

To thee I'll return, overburdened with care;
The heart's dearest solace will smile on me there;
No more from that cottage again will I roam;
Be it ever so humble, there's no place like home.
    Home, home, sweet, sweet home!
There's no place like home, oh, there's no place like home!

JOHN HOWARD PAYNE

THE BLUE BOWL

Reward

All day I did the little things,
The little things that do not show;
I brought the kindling for the fire
I set the candles in a row,
I filled a bowl with marigolds,
The shallow bowl you love the best—
And made the house a pleasant place
Where weariness might take its rest.

The hours sped on, my eager feet
Could not keep pace with my desire.
So much to do, so little time!
I could not let my body tire;
Yet, when the coming of the night
Blotted the garden from my sight,
And on the narrow, gravelled walks
Between the guarding flower stalks
I heard your step: I was not through
With services I meant for you.

You came into the quiet room
That glowed enchanted with the bloom
Of yellow flame. I saw your face,
Illumined by the firelit space,
Slowly grow still and comforted—
"It's good to be at home," you said.

BLANCHE BANE KUDER

THE HONOURS OF HOMEMAKING

No piled-up wealth, no splendour of material growth, no brilliance of
artistic development, will permanently avail any people unless its home
life is healthy, unless the average man possesses honesty, courage,
common-sense and decency, unless he works hard and is willing at
need to fight hard; and unless the average woman is a good wife, a
good mother, able and willing to perform the first and greatest duty
of womanhood, able and willing to bear, and to bring up as they should
be brought up, healthy children, sound in body, mind and character,
and numerous enough so that the race shall increase and not decrease. . . .

Just as the happiest and most honourable and most useful task that can
be set by any man is to earn enough for the support of his wife and
family, for the bringing up and starting in life of his children, so the
most important, the most honourable and desirable task which can be
set by any woman is to be a good and wise mother in a home marked
by self-respect and mutual forbearance.

THEODORE ROOSEVELT

GOD AND HOME AND COUNTRY

"Give me an humble heart that I may see
    What God and home and country mean to me.
I know the beauty of my native land,
    Its quiet hills; its mountains crowned with snow;
Its waters that shall make a desert bloom
    With strangest loveliness; all this I know.

And I have learned of men who gave their lives
  In service that a dream might be fulfilled.
Remembered words have echoed down the years
  A song of freedom that shall not be stilled.
Nor have I quite forgotten that much blood
  Upon the land, a seeping, staining red,
Must be a mark of covenant between
  The valiant living and heroic dead.
And yet it would be well if, for a day,
  My life could be a sharper contrast shown
Against a background, sombre and austere,
  Deprived of all the sunlight I have known
Because, perhaps, I take as if by right
  Unnumbered blessings, scarcely giving heed
Or thanks to that vast fellowship of men
  That, by the grace of God, has met each need.
Too flippantly I speak of sacred things;
  In every diamond I see a flaw.
Too carelessly I tread on Holy ground
  Forgetting to remove my shoes in awe.
Forgive me: clear my vision till I see
  What God and home and country mean to me!

EDGAR A. JONAS

THE HOME

What makes a nation great? Would you say its high raised battlements? Would you say its great national capital?—its well filled treasures of glittering gold and shining silver?—its stocks and bonds that indicate a teeming nation's wealth and power? Would you say its churches?—its cathedrals?—its temples?—and architectural wonder? Would you say its fertile fields?—its mines?—and splendid forests? I would say: "*Yes*," these are an evidence of a nation's wealth, power and prosperity. But, this alone does not constitute a nation's greatness or make a nation great.

The true greatness of a nation is in its homes; the unity of man and woman in the home. The true greatness of a nation is based upon the homes of the nation. The home is the foundation of the government; from it issues the real strength of a nation.

The home is the castle of the average man—the bulwark of the nation. The dweller there—be he humble or otherwise—one who loves his home, his family, his country—these are they that make a nation great. A country filled with homes—the homes of the average man, where mother is divine—at the altar where children are taught to reverence God and respect the laws of their country—this, and this alone, makes a nation truly great. This is a nation of the average man!

ANDERSON M. BATEN

Love of Country

Be faithful to your country, and prefer its dignity and honour to any degree of popularity and honour for yourself; consulting its interest rather than your own, and rather than the pleasure and gratification of the people, which are often at variance with their welfare.

The true Mason identifies the honour of his country with his own. Nothing more conduces to the beauty and glory of one's country than the preservation against all enemies of its civil and religious liberty. The world will never willingly let die the names of those patriots who in her different ages have received upon their own breasts the blows aimed by insolent enemies at the bosom of their country.

But it also conduces, and in no small measure, to the beauty and glory of one's country, that justice should be always administered there to all alike, and neither denied, sold, or delayed to any one.

And he who labours, often against reproach and obloquy, and oftener against indifference and apathy, to bring about that fortunate condition of things when that great code of divine law shall be everywhere and punctually obeyed, is no less a patriot than he who bares his bosom to the hostile steel in the ranks of his country's soldiery.

For Fortitude is not only seen resplendent on the field of battle and amid the clash of arms, but he displays its energy under every difficulty and against every assailant. He who wars against cruelty, oppression, and hoary abuses, fights for his country's honour, which these things soil; and her honour is as important as her existence. Often, indeed, the warfare against those abuses which disgrace one's country is quite as hazardous and more discouraging than that against her enemies in the field; and merits equal, if not greater reward.

Defend weakness against strength, the friendless against the great, the oppressed against the Oppressor! Be ever vigilant and watchful of the interests and honour of your country! and may the Grand Architect of the Universe give you that strength and wisdom which shall enable you well and faithfully to perform these high duties!

ALBERT PIKE

BREATHES THERE THE MAN

Breathes there the man with soul so dead
Who never to himself hath said,
   This is my own, my native land!
Whose heart hath ne'er within him burned,
As home his footsteps he hath turned
   From wandering on a foreign strand?
If such there breathe, go, mark him well;
For him no minstrel raptures swell;
High though his titles, proud his name,
Boundless his wealth as wish can claim.
Despite those titles, power, and pelf,
The wretch, concentred all in self,
Living, shall forfeit fair renown,
And, doubly dying, shall go down
To the vile dust from whence he sprung,
Unwept, unhonoured, and unsung.

SIR WALTER SCOTT

OUR BRETHREN AT THE FRONT

God of our Fathers, at Whose call,
We now before Thine altar fall;
Whose grace can make our Order strong,
Through love of right and hate of wrong,
   We pray Thee in Thy pity shield
   Our Brethren on the battlefield.

Asleep, beneath Thine ample dome,
With many a tender dream of home;
Or charging, in the dust and glare,
With bullets hurtling through the air,
   We pray Thee in Thy pity shield
   Our Brethren on the battlefield.

O soon, Thou Blessed Prince of Peace,
Bring in the days when War shall cease,
And men and brothers shall unite
To fill the world with love and light,
   We pray Thee in Thy pity shield
   Our Brethren on the battlefield.

ANONYMOUS

The man who loves his country on its own account and not merely for its trappings of interest or power, can never be divorced from it, can never refuse to come forward when he finds that she is engaged in dangers which he has the means of warding off.

THOMAS JEFFERSON

It is the duty of every citizen to serve his State whenever called upon to do so, and his sole reward should be the consciousness of having fulfilled that obligation. If my fellow-citizens think that I have ever been able to serve my State in any manner, I only discharged my duty in doing so and am amply compensated for any services rendered by their verdict of "Well done, good and faithful servant."

WADE HAMPTON

To preserve the peace of our fellow citizens, promote their prosperity and happiness, reunite opinion, cultivate a spirit of candour, moderation, charity and forbearance toward one another, are objects calling for the efforts and sacrifices of every good man and patriot. Our religion enjoins it; our happiness demands it; and no sacrifice is requisite but of passions hostile to both.

THOMAS JEFFERSON

If men were angels, no government would be necessary. If angels were to govern men, neither external nor internal controls on government would be necessary. In framing a government which is to be administered by men over men, the great difficulty lies in this: You must first enable the government to control the governed; and in the next place oblige it to control itself.

GEORGE WASHINGTON

No man has ever appeared upon the theatre of human action whose integrity was more incorruptible, or whose principles were more perfectly free from the contamination of those selfish and unworthy passions which find their nourishment in the conflicts of party. His ends were always upright, and his means always pure. He exhibits the rare example of a politician to whom wiles were absolutely unknown. In him was fully exemplified the real distinction between wisdom and cunning, and the truth of the maxim that "honesty is the best policy."

Neither the extraordinary partiality of the American people, the extravagant praises which were bestowed upon him, nor the inveterate opposition and malignant calumnies which he encountered, had any visible influence on his conduct.

JOHN MARSHALL

COUNSEL

Long as thine Art shall love true love,
  Long as thy Science truth shall know,
Long as thine Eagle harms no Dove,
  Long as thy Law by law shall grow,
Long as thy God is God above,
  Thy brother every man below,
So long, dear Land of all my love,
  Thy name shall shine, thy fame shall glow.

SIDNEY LANIER

I only regret that I have but one life to lose for my country.

NATHAN HALE

Our country! In her intercourse with foreign nations may she always be in the right; but our country, right or wrong.

STEPHEN DECATUR

Ever since I arrived at the state of manhood and acquainted myself with the general history of mankind, I have felt a sincere passion for liberty. The history of nations, doomed to perpetual slavery, in consequence of yielding up to tyrants their natural-born liberties, I read with a sort of philosophical horror; so that the first systematical and bloody attempt, at Lexington, to enslave America, thoroughly electrified my mind and fully determined me to take part with my country.

ETHAN ALLEN

As a man and citizen the poet will love his fatherland, but the fatherland of his poetic powers and his poetic activity is the good, the noble, the beautiful, which is the property of no particular province and no particular land. This he seizes upon and forms wherever he finds it. In this he is like the eagle that lets its eye roam freely over the lands and cares not whether the hare upon which it swoops is running in Prussia or in Saxony.

And what does it mean to love one's fatherland, and what does it mean to be patriotically active? If a poet has endeavoured all his life to fight harmful prejudice, to eliminate narrowness, to enlighten the spirit of his people, to purify their taste, and to ennoble their sentiments, what is there better for him to do? And how is he to be more patriotically alive? To put such improper and thankless demands to a poet is as though one were to require of a general that to be a proper patriot he should get involved in political reforms and neglect his immediate duties. But the fatherland of a general is his regiment, and he will be an excellent patriot if he pays no attention to political matters except in so far as they concern him, rather devoting all his thought and care to the battalions under his command, seeking to drill and train them so well that if someday the fatherland is endangered they will not flinch in the face of the enemy.

I hate all botchwork like sin, but especially botching in affairs of state, which leads to nothing but harm for thousands and millions.

JOHANN WOLFGANG VON GOETHE

From THE SHIP OF STATE

Thou, too, sail on, O ship of State!
Sail on, O Union, strong and great!
Humanity with all its fears,
With all its hopes of future years,
Is hanging breathless on thy fate!
We know what Master laid thy keel,
What workmen wrought thy ribs of steel,

Who made each mast, and sail, and rope,
What anvils rang, what hammers beat,
In what a forge and what a heat
Were shaped the anchors of thy hope!
Fear not each sudden sound and shock,
'Tis of the wave and not the rock;
'Tis but the flapping of the sail,
And not a rent made by the gale!
In spite of rock and tempest's roar,
In spite of false lights on the shore,
Sail on, nor fear to breast the sea!
Our hearts, our hopes, are all with thee,
Our hearts, our hopes, our prayers, our tears,
Our faith, triumphant o'er our fears,
Are all with thee,—are all with thee!

HENRY WADSWORTH LONGFELLOW

"If you are ever tempted to say a word or do a thing that should put a bar between you and your family, your home, and your country, pray God in His Mercy to take you that instant home to His own heaven. Stick by your family, boy; forget you have a self, while you do everything for them. Think of your home, boy; write and send, and talk about it. Let it be nearer and nearer to your thought, the farther you have to travel from it; and rush back to it, when you are free. And for your country, boy, and that flag, never dream a dream but serving her as she bids you, though the service carry you through a thousand hells. No matter what happens to you, not matter who flatters or who abuses you, never look at another flag, never let a night pass but you pray God to bless that flag. Remember that behind all these men you have to deal with, behind officers, and government, and people even, there is the Country Herself, your country, and that you belong to her as you belong to your own mother. Stand by her, boy, as you would stand by your own mother."

EDWARD EVERETT HALE

And let the sacred obligations which have devolved on this generation, and on us, sink deep into our hearts. Those who established our liberty and our government are daily dropping from among us. The great trust now descends to new hands. Let us apply ourselves to that which is presented to us, as our appropriate object . . . There remains to us a great duty of defence and preservation; and there is opened to us, also, a noble pursuit, to which the spirit of the times strongly invites us. Our proper business is improvement. Let our age be the age of improvement. In a day of peace, let us advance the arts of peace and the works of peace. Let us develop the resources of our land, call forth its powers, build up its institutions, promote all its great interests, and see whether we also, in our day and generation, may not perform something worthy to be remembered. Let us cultivate a true spirit of union and harmony. In pursuing the great objects which our condition points out to us, let us act under a settled conviction, and an habitual feeling, that these States are one country. Let our conceptions be enlarged to the circle of our duties. Let us extend our ideas over the whole vast field in which we are called to act. Let our object be, OUR COUNTRY, OUR WHOLE COUNTRY, AND NOTHING BUT OUR COUNTRY. And by the blessing of God, may that country itself become a vast and splendid monument, not of oppression and terror, but of Wisdom, of Peace, and of Liberty, upon which the world may gaze with admiration for ever.

DANIEL WEBSTER

SUPPORT OF GOVERNMENT

So far as I am acquainted with the principles and doctrines of Freemasonry, I conceive it to be founded in benevolence and to be exercised only for the good of mankind . . .

At this important and critical moment, when repeated and high indignities have been offered to this government, your country and the rights and properties of our citizens plundered without a prospect of redress, I conceive to be the indispensible duty of every American, let his situation and circumstances be what they may, to come forward in support of the Government of his country and to give all the aid in his power toward maintaining that independence which we have so dearly purchased; and under this impression, I did not hesitate to lay aside all personal considerations and accept my appointment.

GEORGE WASHINGTON

The Masonic Fraternity does not put the primary emphasis on the nation, important as that is. Patriotism is one of the loveliest things in the world—love of one's own; the thing that makes people who were born by the sea lonely without the sound of the sea in their ears; or makes those brought up in the forests or mountains feel almost naked if away from their comforting shadows; or makes people who like myself were born out on the plains, feel hemmed in and cramped in the roaring city. Love of one's own is good. But if it becomes uncritical loyalty to one's own exclusively, then it divides instead of unites. There are some 80 or 90 nations and if you say, "First, my nation," then you must grant that right to others, and you cannot get a united world.

The Masonic Fraternity does not even put the primary emphasis on creed or sect, because they also divide.

I ask you, what is the one thing we all have in common? It is just this: our common humanity. And that is where the Craft puts the primary emphasis, on the one thing we all have in common. Next to God, it puts the primary emphasis on the individual human being—his worth and his welfare.

This immediately gives hope, because it deals with that which can be changed. Governments, as such, do not have consciences. Institutions, as such, are not self-critical. But a man can respond to a "still, small voice," and be changed. The history of changed governments and institutions and societies is the history of changed men.

God spoke to a layman who was a political refugee, an old man, his career finished, hiding for his life in the mountains, tending sheep. And the Lord said, "Moses, go down into Egypt and get my people." And the history of the world was changed, because the man was changed.

God spoke to another layman on the way to Damascus. Not only was he perfectly correct himself under the law, but he was policing everybody else's actions as well. And the Lord said, "Saul, Saul, why persecutest thou me?" The man went for a week-end to a "layman's retreat," and had some wise counsel from the clergy, and he came out a different individual.

God spoke to a boy down in New Orleans' slave auction mart, and the young lad grit his teeth and said, "If the time ever comes when I can strike this traffic in human beings, I will strike with all my strength." Abraham Lincoln changed the history of the world.

This world is too sick to be patched up with superficial plasters. Only an Almighty and loving Father, working through changed men, through us, His sons, can save this broken, divided world, and make of it the united peaceful force it must be.

This is a day of judgment on yesterday; it is also a day of decision for tomorrow. As long as men trusted in their own smart plans and clever schemes, there was no hope. Those have come to naught. It is a day for us to lift up our hearts. I am hopeful today because we are beginning to be hopeless about ourselves—for that gives God His chance.

WALTER H. JUDD

THE ETERNAL REMEMBRANCE OF THE BRAVE

Make the daily-increasing grandeur of this community the object of your thoughts and grow quite enamoured of it. And, when it really appears great to your apprehensions think again, that this grandeur was acquired by brave and valiant men; by men who knew their duty, and in the moments of action were sensible of shame; who, whenever their attempts were unsuccessful, thought it dishonour their country should stand in need of anything their valour could do for it, and so made it the most glorious present. Bestowing thus their lives on the public, they have every one received a praise that will never decay, a sepulchre that will always be most illustrious—not that in which their bones lie mouldering, but that in which their fame is preserved, to be on every occasion, when honour is the employ of either word or act, eternally remembered. This whole earth is the sepulchre of illustrious men; nor is it the inscription on the columns in their native soil alone that shews their merit, but the memorial of them, better than all inscriptions, in every foreign nation, reposited more durably in universal remembrance, than on their own tomb.

THUCYDIDES

A Blessed Immortality

In the democracy of death all men are at last equal. There is neither rank, nor station, nor prerogative in the republic of the grave. At this fatal threshold the philospher ceases to be wise, and the songs of the poet are silent. Dives relinquishes his millions and Lazarus his rags. The poor man is as rich as the richest, and the rich man is as poor as the pauper. The creditor loses his usury and the debtor is acquitted of his obligations. There the proud man surrenders his dignities, the politician his honours, the worldling his pleasures, the individual needs no physician and the labourer rests from his unrequited toil. Here, at last is nature's final equity. The wrongs of time are redressed, injustice is explained, the irony of fate is refuted, the unequal distribution of wealth, honour, capacity, pleasure and opportunity, which makes life so cruel and inexplicable a tragedy, cease in the realms of death. The strongest has no supremacy and the weakest needs no defence. The mighty captain succumbs to the invincible adversary, who disarms alike the victor and the vanquished.

JOHN J. INGALLS

THE APRON SYMBOLISM

More ancient than the Golden Fleece
  Whose story shines in classic lore:
Or Roman Eagle—which portrayed
  Chivalric deeds in days of yore.

More honoured than the Knightly Star,
  Or Royal Garter, it must be;
A symbol you should fondly keep
  From spot and stain forever free.

It may be that in coming years,
    As time shall all your labours test:
That laurel leaves of Victory
    Shall on your brow in honour rest.

Yea, from your breast may jewels hang
    Fit any diadem to grace:
And sparkling gems of beauty rare
    May on your person find a place.

Nay more, perchance with coming light,
    Your feet may tread the path of fame:
Which in our Mystic order leads
    To glory, and an honoured name.

Yes, on your shoulders there may rest
    The purple which we hold so dear:
That ensign which our progress marks
    In high fraternal circles here.

But never more can you receive
    From mortal hand while here below:
An emblem which such honour brings
    As this one—which I now bestow.

Until your spirit shall have passed
    Beyond the pearly gates above:
May this the "Badge of Innocence"
    Remind you of your vows of love.

'Tis yours to wear throughout your life,
    'Till death shall call your soul to God:
Then on your casket to be placed,
    When you shall sleep beneath the sod.

Its spotless surface is a type
    Of that which marks a noble mind:
The rectitude of heart and life,
    Which in its teachings you should find.

And when at last your weary feet
  Shall reach the goal awaiting all:
And from your tired nerveless grasp
  The working tools of life shall fall.

May then the record of your life,
  Reflect the pure and spotless white
Of this fair token which I place
  Within your keeping here tonight.

And as your naked soul shall stand
  Before the great white throne of light;
And judgment for the deeds of earth
  Shall issue there—to bless or blight;

Then may you hear the Welcome Voice
  That tells of endless joys begun,
As God shall own your faithfulness,
  And greet you with the words, "Well Done."

NEAL A. MCAULAY

HIGH FLIGHT

Oh! I have slipped the surly bonds of Earth
And danced the skies on laughter-silvered wings;
Sunward I've climbed, and joined the tumbling mirth
Of sun-split clouds—and done a hundred things
You have not dreamed of—wheeled and soared and swung
High in the sunlit silence. Hov'ring there,
I've chased the shouting wind along, and flung
My eager craft through footless halls of air . . . .
Up, up the long, delirious, burning blue
I've topped the wind-swept heights with easy grace.
Where never lark, or even eagle, flew;
And, while with silent, lifting mind I've trod
The high untrespassed sanctity of space,
Put out my hand, and touched the face of God.

JOHN GILLESPIE MAGEE, JR.

247

IMMORTALITY

If the father deigns to touch with divine power the cold and pulseless heart of the buried acorn and to make it burst forth from its prison walls, will he leave neglected in the earth the soul of man, made in the image of his Creator? If he stoops to whisper to the rosebush whose withered blossoms float upon the autumn breeze the sweet assurance of another springtime, will he refuse the words of hope to the sons of men when the frosts of winter come? If matter, mute and inanimate, though changed by the forces of nature into a multitude of forms, can never die, will the spirit of man suffer annihilation when it has paid a brief visit like a royal guest to this tenement of clay? No, I am as sure that there is another life as I am that I live today!

In Cairo I secured a few grains of wheat that had slumbered for more than three thousand years in an Egyptian tomb; as I looked at them this thought came into my mind: If one of those grains had been planted on the banks of the river Nile the year after it grew, and all its lineal descendants planted and replanted from that time until now, its progeny would be sufficiently numerous to feed the teeming millions of the world. There is in the grain of wheat an invisible something which has power to discard the body we see, and from earth and air fashion a new body so much like the old one that we cannot tell the one from the other. If this invisible germ of life in the grain of wheat can thus pass unimpaired through three thousand resurrections, I shall not doubt that my soul has power to clothe itself with a body suited to its new existence when this earthly frame has crumbled into dust.

WILLIAM JENNINGS BRYAN

I cannot tell you when the idea of a Soul in every man had its origin. Most likely the first parents brought it with them out of the garden in which they had their first dwelling. We all do know, however, that it has never perished entirely out of mind. By some peoples it was lost, but not by all; in some ages it dulled and faded; in others it was overwhelmed with doubts; but, in great goodness, God kept sending us at intervals mighty intellects to argue it back to faith and hope.

Why should there be a Soul in every man? For one moment look at the necessity for such a device. To lie down and die, and be no more—no more forever—time never was when man wished for such an end; nor has the man even been who did not in his heart promise himself something better. The monuments of the nations are all protests against nothingness after death; so are statues and inscriptions; so is history.

Ask you what God's plan is? The gift of a Soul to each of us at birth, with this simple law—there shall be no immortality except through the Soul. . . .

A word as to the pleasure there is in the thought of a Soul in each of us. In the first place, it robs death of its terrors by making dying a change for the better, and burial but the planting of a seed from which there will spring a new life. What happiness in the promise that when the tomb opens to receive the work-out husk I call myself, the now viewless doors of the universe, which is but the palace of God, will swing ajar to receive me, a liberated immortal Soul!

I would I could tell you the ecstasy there must be in that life to come! Do not say I know nothing about it. This much I know, and it is enough for me—the being a Soul implies conditions of divine superiority. In such a being there is no dust, nor any gross thing; it must be finer than air, more impalpable than light, purer than essence— it is life in absolute purity.

Knowing so much, shall I dispute with myself or you about the unnecessaries—about the form of my soul? Or where it is to abide? Or whether it eats and drinks? Or is winged, or wears this or that? No. It is more becoming to trust in God. The beautiful in this world is all from his hand declaring the perfection of taste; he is the author of all form; he clothes the lily, he colours the rose, he distils the dew-drop, he makes the music of nature; in a word, he organized us for this life, and imposed its conditions; and they are such guaranty to me that, trustful as a little child, I leave to him the organization of my Soul, and every arrangement for the life after death. I know he loves me.

LEW WALLACE

WE TAKE THOSE THINGS WE GAVE AWAY

Our Lord created everything with spiritual design
And as we live the more we see His plan was most divine.
We fail at times to trust in Him—and often bank on hopeless
    schemes
When suddenly we realize there's nothing left but faded dreams.
As time goes marching on we learn there's only one enchanted
    road
The path is straight—it may seem long when burdened with a
    heavy load

But once we reach the distant goal and gaze upon the setting sun
We feel the trip was worth the toll—T'was but a trial—a task
    well done
The moral is keep travelling on—do something worthy every
    day.
Remember when we leave this earth—We Take Those Things
    We Gave Away.

ABRAHAM FELT

NOW THE LABOURER'S TASK IS O'ER

Now the labourer's task is o'er;
  Now the battle day is past;
Now upon the farther shore
  Lands the voyager at last.
Father, in thy gracious keeping
Leave we now thy servant sleeping.

There the tears of earth are dried;
  There its hidden things are clear;
There the work of life is tried
  By a juster Judge than here.
Father, in thy gracious keeping
Leave we now thy servant sleeping.

There the sinful souls, that turn
  To the cross their dying eyes,
All the love of Christ shall learn
  At his feet in Paradise.
Father, in thy gracious keeping
Leave we now thy servant sleeping.

"Earth to earth, and dust to dust,"
  Calmly now the words we say;
Left behind, we wait in trust
  For the resurrection day.
Father, in thy gracious keeping
Leave we now thy servant sleeping.

JOHN ELLERTON

IMMORTALITY

It is useless to try to prove by logic or by demonstration the immortality of man. We believe it, there is an end to it! And we do not believe it because we have proved it but we try to prove it because we already believe it. It is hope, a kind of inward certainty which finds its support not in this fact or in that, but in the cast and colour of life as a whole. It rises up into our minds like an exaltation from all our thoughts, all our experiences, all our dreams, as the odour that drifts across a summer field distils from numberless unnoted plants. We are never so puzzled as when we are challenged to give a reasoned proof of this hope; and we are never so unreasonable as when we cease to believe it. Men everywhere and always have believed it not because priests have taught them or because scientists have found out the secret of it, but because life itself has taught them, and it is something that the universe itself is always whispering to them.

H. L. HAYWOOD

Since death is the true end and object of life, I have so accustomed myself to this true best friend of man, that its image not only has no terrors for me but tranquilizes and comforts me. And here I thank God that he has given me the opportunity of knowing it as the key of all beatitude.

WOLFGANG AMADEUS MOZART

PROSPICE

Fear death?—to feel the fog in my throat,
    The mist in my face,
When the snows begin, and the blasts denote
    I am nearing the place,
The power of the night, the press of the storm,
    The post of the foe;
Where he stands, the Arch Fear in a visible form,
    Yet the strong man must go:
For the journey is done and the summit attained,
    And the barriers fall,
Though a battle's to fight ere the guerdon be gained,
    The reward of it all.

I was ever a fighter, so—one fight more,
   The best and the last!
I would hate that death bandaged my eyes, and forebore,
   And bade me creep past.
No! let me taste the whole of it, fare like my peers
   The heroes of old,
Bear the brunt, in a minute pay glad life's arrears
   Of pain, darkness and cold.
For sudden the worst turns the best to the brave,
   The black minute's at end,
And the elements' rage, the fiend-voices that rave,
   Shall dwindle, shall blend,
Shall change, shall become first a peace out of pain,
   Then a light, then thy breast,
O thou soul of my soul! I shall clasp thee again,
   And with God be the rest!

ROBERT BROWNING

LIFE'S IMMORTALITY

Life is immortal. It has outlived eons and geologic ages. Continents
have arisen and been submerged. The ancient oceans and the shallow
seas teemed with life. It sounds the depths; it permeates the crest of
the breaking wave and the sands of every shore. It has advanced with
every great retreat of every ice age; vigorous and undefeated, it has
resisted each frigid advance. Mountains have arisen from the wrinkled
earth, the surface has cracked and trembled with the quake. The record
of millions of years of erosion that erased the mountains' vast height
is shown, strata on strata. The continents have been washed into the
sea. The silt of the ancient land, like a shroud, veils the bottom of
every ocean, but life has survived. . . .

Life is a sculptor and shapes all living things; an artist that designs
every leaf of every tree, that colours the flowers, the apple, the forest,
and the plumage of the bird of paradise. Life is a musician and has
taught each bird to sing its love songs, the insects to call each other
in the music of their multitudinous sounds. . . .

What life is no man has yet fathomed; it has no weight or dimen-
sions. Life has force, for a growing root will crack a rock. Life builds

a mighty tree and holds it against gravity for a thousand years or more. It lifts tons of water from the earth each day and builds the leaves and fruits. The oldest living thing is a tree, and this covers a span of five thousand years—a moment in eternity. So individual life is fleeting. Life accounts for every motion of every living thing. . . .

Life is the only source of consciousness and it alone makes possible knowledge of the works of GOD which we, still half-blind, yet know to be good. Life is an instrumentality serving the purposes of the Supreme Intelligence. LIFE IS IMMORTAL.

A. CRESSY MORRISON

"I CANNOT THINK OF THEM AS DEAD"

I cannot think of them as dead
  Who walk with me no more;
Along the path of life I tread
  They have but gone before.

The Father's house is mansioned fair
  Beyond my vision dim;
All souls are his, and here or there
  Are living unto him.

And still their silent ministry
  Within my heart hath place,
As when on earth they walked with me
  And met me face to face.

Their lives are made forever mine;
  What they to me have been
Hath left henceforth its seal and sign
  Engraven deep within.

Mine are they by an ownership
  Nor time nor death can free;
For God hath given to love to keep
  Its own eternally.

FREDERICK LUCIAN HOSMER

253

REASONS FOR IMMORTALITY

For my part I find the world is good. It is a most reliable paymaster, whichever way you make your investment, and I am glad to be in it. Everything seems to have a purpose, and from that fact I deduce a purposer. The world seems reasonable, and therefore likely to end reasonably. The evolution of love, the development of intellect, the unceasing metabolism of the body, considered with the principle of the conservation of energy, always seems to me to argue against the annihilation of personality. Some men hate the whole universe because they realize how brief the tenure of the things they love in life is. But I am no pessimist. Knowing that I can only stay here for a brief time alongside of what I call my property, I am still delighted with all I get, enjoying immensely the use of it while I have it, and believing, as Christ teaches, that so-called death cannot rob me of spiritual friendships and assets. If I count what I can contribute to life, and not what I can get out of it, that of itself makes it worth while. The gauge is not what we have, but what we do with what we have.

I am as sure that I am not my body as I am sure that I am not my house. But for all that, I know that I am I, and that I shall always continue to be so is sufficiently probable to satisfy me.

SIR WILFRED GRENFELL

THEY SOFTLY WALK

They are not gone who pass
Beyond the clasp of hand,
Out from the strong embrace.
They are but come so close
We need not grope with hands,
Nor look to see, nor try
To catch the sound of feet.
They have put off their shoes
Softly to walk by day
Within our thoughts, to tread
At night our dream-led paths
Of sleep.

They are not lost who find
The sunset gate, the goal
Of all their faithful years.
Not lost are they who reach
The summit of their climb,
The peak above the clouds
And storms. They are not lost
Who find the light of sun
And stars and God.

They are not dead who live
In hearts they leave behind.
In those whom they have blessed
They live a life again,
And shall live through the years
Eternal life, and grow
Each day more beautiful
As time declares their good,
Forgets the rest, and proves
Their immortality.

HUGH ROBERT ORR

They that love beyond the world cannot be separated by it. Death
cannot kill what never dies, nor can spirits ever be divided that love
and live in the same divine principle. . . . . Death is but crossing the
world, as friends do the seas; they live in one another still.

WILLIAM PENN

THE FIVE POINTS OF SYMBOLISM

Foot to foot that we may go,
Where our help we can bestow;
Pointing out the better way,
Lest our brothers go astray.
　　Thus our steps should always lead
　　To the souls that are in need.

Knee to knee, that we may share
Every brother's needs in prayer:
Giving all his wants a place,
When we seek the throne of grace.
  In our thoughts from day to day
  For each other we should pray.

Breast to breast, to there conceal,
What our lips must not reveal;
When a brother does confide,
We must by his will abide.
  Mason's secrets to us known,
  We must cherish as our own.

Hand to back, our love to show
To the brother, bending low:
Underneath a load of care,
Which we may and ought to share.
  That the weak may always stand,
  Let us lend a helping hand.

Cheek to cheek, or mouth to ear,
That our lips may whisper cheer,
To our brother in distress:
Whom our words can aid and bless.
  Warn him if he fails to see,
  Dangers that are known to thee.

Foot to foot, and knee to knee,
Breast to breast, as brothers we:
Hand to back and mouth to ear,
Then that mystic word we hear,
  Which we otherwise conceal,
  But on these five points reveal.

NEAL A. MCAULAY

MR. VALIANT-FOR-TRUTH

When the day he was to be gone was come, he addressed himself to
go over the river. Now the river at that time overflowed its banks in

some places; but Mr. Honest in his life-time had spoken to one Good-Conscience to meet him there; the which he also did, and lent him his hand and so helped him over. The last words of Mr. Honest were 'Grace reigns': so he left the world. After this it was noised abroad that Mr. Valiant-for-Truth was taken with a summons by the same post as the other, and had this for a token that the summons was true, that his pitcher was broken at the fountain. When he understood it, he called for his friends and told them of it. Then said he, I am going to my Father's; and though with great difficulty I have got hither, yet now I do not repent me all the trouble I have been at to arrive where I am. My sword I give to him that shall succeed me in my pilgrimage, and my courage and skill to him that can get it. My marks and scars I carry with me, to be a witness for me that I have fought his battles, who now will be my rewarder. When the day that he must go hence was come, many accompanied him to the river-side; into which as he went he said, Death, where is thy sting? And as he went down deeper he said, Grave, where is thy victory? So he passed over, and all the trumpets sounded for him on the other side.

JOHN BUNYAN

LAST LINES

No coward soul is mine,
No trembler in the world's storm-troubled sphere:
  I see Heaven's glories shine,
And faith shines equal, arming me from fear.

  O God within my breast,
Almighty, ever-present Deity!
  Life—that in me has rest,
As I—undying Life—have power in Thee!

  Vain are the thousand creeds
That move men's hearts: unutterably vain;
  Worthless as wither'd weeds,
Or idlest froth amid the boundless main,

  To waken doubt in one
Holding so fast by thine infinity;
  So surely anchor'd on
The steadfast rock of immortality.

With wide-embracing love
Thy Spirit animates eternal years,
   Pervades and broods above,
Changes, sustains, dissolves, creates, and rears.

   Though earth and man were gone,
And suns and universes ceased to be,
   And Thou were left alone,
Every existence would exist in Thee.

   There is not room for Death,
Nor atom that his might could render void:
   Thou—Thou art Being and Breath,
And what Thou art may never be destroy'd.

EMILY BRONTË

THERE IS NO DEATH

There is a plan far greater than the plan you know;
There is a landscape broader than the one you see.
There is a haven where storm-tossed souls may go—
You call it death—we, immortality.

You call it death—this seeming endless sleep;
We call it birth—the soul at last set free.
'Tis hampered not by time or space—you weep.
Why weep at death? 'Tis immortality.

Farewell, dear voyageur—'twill not be long.
Your work is done—now may peace rest with thee.
Your kindly thoughts and deeds—they will live on.
This is not death—'tis immortality.

Farewell, dear voyageur—the river winds and turns;
The cadence of your song wafts near to me,
And now you know the thing that all men learn:
There is no death—there's immortality.

ANONYMOUS

We all know that something is eternal. And it ain't houses and it ain't names, and it ain't earth, and it ain't even the stars—everybody knows in their bones that something is eternal, and that something has to do with human beings. All the greatest people ever lived have been telling us that for five thousand years and yet you'd be surprised how people are always letting go of that fact. There's something way down deep that's eternal about every human being.

THORNTON WILDER

HAMLET'S SOLILOQUY

To be, or not to be: that is the question:
Whether 'tis nobler in the mind to suffer
The slings and arrows of outrageous fortune,
Or to take arms against a sea of troubles,
And by opposing end them? To die: to sleep;
No more; and, by a sleep to say we end
The heart-ache and the thousand natural shocks
That flesh is heir to, 'tis a consummation
Devoutly to be wish'd. To die, to sleep;
To sleep: perchance to dream: ay, there's the rub;
For in that sleep of death what dreams may come
When we have shuffled off this mortal coil,
Must give us pause. There's the respect
That makes calamity of so long life;
For who would bear the whips and scorns of time,
The oppressor's wrong, the proud man's contumely,
The pangs of despis'd love, the law's delay,
The insolence of office, and the spurns
That patient merit of the unworthy takes,
When he himself might his quietus make
With a bare bodkin? who would fardels bear,
To grunt and sweat under a weary life,
But that the dread of something after death,
The undiscover'd country from whose bourn
No traveller returns, puzzles the will,
And makes us rather bear those ills we have
Than fly to others that we know not of?
Thus conscience does make cowards of us all;

And thus the native hue of resolution
Is sicklied o'er with the pale cast of thought,
And enterprises of great pith and moment
With this regard their currents turn awry,
And lose the name of action.

WILLIAM SHAKESPEARE

I still have enjoyment in the company of my friends; and, being easy in my circumstances, have many reasons to like living. But the course of nature must soon put a period to my present mode of existence. This I shall submit to with less regret, as having seen, during a long life, a good deal of this world, I feel a growing curiosity to be acquainted with some other; and can cheerfully, with filial confidence, resign my spirit to the conduct of that great and good Parent of mankind who created it, and who has so graciously protected and prospered me from my birth to the present hour.

BENJAMIN FRANKLIN

COWARDS

Cowards die many times before their deaths:
The valiant never taste of death but once.
Of all the wonders that I yet have heard,
It seems to me most strange that men should fear;
Seeing that death, a necessary end,
Will come, when it will come.

WILLIAM SHAKESPEARE

From MORTE D'ARTHUR

"The old order changeth, yielding place to new,
And God fulfils himself in many ways,
Lest one good custom should corrupt the world.
Comfort thyself: what comfort is in me!
I have lived my life, and that which I have done

May He within himself make pure! but thou,
If thou shouldst never see my face again,
Pray for my soul. More things are wrought by prayer
Than this world dreams of. Wherefore, let thy voice
Rise like a fountain for me night and day.
For what are men better than sheep or goats
That nourish a blind life within the brain,
If, knowing God, they lift not hands of prayer
Both for themselves and those who call them friend?
For so the whole round earth is every way
Bound by gold chains about the feet of God.
But now farewell. I am going a long way
With these thou seest—if indeed I go—
(For all my mind is clouded with a doubt)
To the island-valley of Avilion;
Where falls not hail, or rain, or any snow,
Nor ever wind blows loudly; but it lies
Deep-meadow'd, happy, fair with orchard-lawns
And bowery hollows crown'd with summer sea,
Where I will heal me of my grievous wound."

ALFRED, LORD TENNYSON

Men fear death as children fear to go in the dark. And as that natural fear in children is increased with tales, so is the other. Certainly, the contemplation of death, as the wages of sin and passage to another world, is holy and religious. But the fear of it, as a tribute due unto Nature, is weak . . . It is worthy of the observing that there is no passion in the mind of man so weak but it mates and masters the fear of death. And, therefore, death is no such terrible enemy when a man hath so many attendants about him that can win the combat of him. Revenge triumphs over death. Honour aspireth to it. Grief fleeth to it. Fear preoccupateth it . . . A man would die, though he were neither valiant nor miserable, only upon a weariness to do the same thing so oft over and over. It is no less worthy to observe how little alteration in good spirits the approach of death makes. For they appear to be the same men to the last instant . . . It is as natural to die as to be born; but to a little infant, perhaps, the one is as painful as the other. He that dies in an earnest pursuit is like one that is wounded in hot blood, who, for the time, scarce feels the hurt. And, therefore, a mind fixed and bent upon somewhat that is good doth avert the dolors of death. But above all, believe it, the sweetest canticle is, *Nunc dimittis;* when a man hath obtained worthy ends and expectations. Death hath this also; that it openeth the gate to good fame and extinguisheth envy.

FRANCIS BACON

ARMED

(Quatrains, after Omar)

"The Moving Finger Writes, and have writ. . . ."
So Omar sang, Nor any Jesuit
   Can find the flaw or prove a sophistry,
Showing his wisdom to be counterfeit.

All of life's paths lead to the black-veiled gate.
And only when we pass we see the Fate
   Which with a sword stands well-concealed behind.
When swings the portal wide it is too late.

Before the dim dread Shape we stand aghast,
Dreading his summons. Outer scape is vast
   And we go forth alone and naked. Yet
We hope; he cannot take us from the past.

And in the past, the Mystic Tie. . . . a key
To lock the dreadful door! We make no plea
   But in the Reaper's face our fingers snap!
What should *we* fear, who have known Masonry?

CARL H. CLAUDY

When I go down to the grave I can say, like many others: "I have finished my day's work." But I cannot say: "I have finished my life." My day's work will begin again the next morning. The tomb is not a blind alley; it is a thoroughfare. It closes on the twilight; it opens on the dawn.

VICTOR HUGO

SOME TIME

Some time at eve, when the tide is low,
I shall slip my moorings and sail away
With no response to a friendly hail,
In the silent hush of the twilight pale,
When the night stoops down to embrace the day
And the voices call in the water's flow—
Some time at eve, when the tide is low,
I shall slip my moorings and sail away
Through purple shadows that darkly trail
O'er the ebbing tide of the unknown sea,
And a ripple of waters to tell the tale
Of a lonely voyager, sailing away
To mystic isles, where at anchor lay
The craft of those who have sailed before,
O'er the unknown sea to the unknown shore.
A few who have watched me sail away
Will miss my craft from the busy bay;
Some friendly barks that were anchored near,
Some loving souls that my heart held dear,
In silent sorrow will drop a tear:
But I shall have peacefully furled my sail
In mooring sheltered from storm and gale
And greeting the friends who have sailed before
O'er the unknown sea to the unknown shore.

ANONYMOUS

DEATH AND IMMORTALITY

I believe in the immortality of the soul, not in the sense in which I
accept the demonstrable truths of science, but as a supreme act of
faith in the reasonableness of God's work.

JOHN FISKE

LIFE

Life! I know not what thou art,
But know that thou and I must part;
And when, or how, or where we met
I own to me's a secret yet.

Life! we've been long together,
Through pleasant and through cloudy weather;
'Tis hard to part when friends are dear—
Perhaps 'twill cost a sigh, a tear;
    Then steal away, give little warning,
Choose thine own time;
Say not good night—but in some brighter clime
    Bid me good morning.

ANNA LAETITIA BARBAULD

THE CHOIR INVISIBLE

Oh, may I join the choir invisible
Of those immortal dead who live again
In minds made better by their presence; live
In pulses stirred to generosity,
In deeds of daring rectitude, in scorn
For miserable aims that end with self,
In thoughts sublime that pierce the night like stars,
And with their mild persistence urge men's search
To vaster issues. So to live is heaven:
To make undying music in the world,
Breathing a beauteous order that controls
With growing sway the growing life of man.
So we inherit that sweet purity
For which we struggled, failed, and agonized
With widening retrospect that bred despair.
Rebellious flesh that would not be subdued,
A vicious parent shaming still its child,
Poor anxious penitence, is quick dissolved;
Its discords, quenched by meeting harmonies,
Die in the large and charitable air.
And all our rarer, better, truer self,
That sobbed religiously in yearning song,
That watched to ease the burden of the world,
Laboriously tracing what must be,
And what may yet be better,—saw within
A worthier image for the sanctuary,
And shaped it forth before the multitude,
Divinely human, raising worship so

To higher reverence more mixed with love,—
That better self shall live till human Time
Shall fold its eyelids, and the human sky
Be gathered like a scroll within the tomb
Unread forever. This is the life to come,—
Which martyred men have made more glorious
For us who strive to follow. May I reach
That purest heaven,—be to other souls
That cup of strength in some great agony,
Enkindle generous ardour, feed pure love,
Beget the smiles that have no cruelty—
Be the sweet presence of a good diffused,
And in diffusion even more intense.
So shall I join the choir invisible
Whose music is the gladness of the world.

GEORGE ELIOT

CROSSING THE BAR

Sunset and evening star,
   And one clear call for me!
And may there be no moaning of the bar
   When I put out to sea,

But such a tide as moving seems asleep,
   Too full for sound and foam,
When that which drew from out the boundless deep
   Turns again home.

Twilight and evening bell,
   And after that the dark!
And may there be no sadness of farewell
   When I embark;

For, though from out our bourne of time and place
   The flood may bear me far,
I hope to see my Pilot face to face
   When I have cross'd the bar.

ALFRED, LORD TENNYSON

I die, worshipping God, loving my friends, not hating my enemies, but despising superstition.

VOLTAIRE

So live, that when thy summons comes to join
The innumerable caravan, which moves
To that mysterious realm, where each shall take
His chamber in the silent halls of death,
Thou go not, like the quarry-slave at night,
Scourged to his dungeon, but, sustained and soothed
By an unfaltering trust, approach thy grave
Like one who wraps the drapery of his couch
About him, and lies down to pleasant dreams.

WILLIAM CULLEN BRYANT

REQUIEM

Under the wide and starry sky
Dig the grave and let me lie,
Glad did I live and gladly die,
And I lay me down with a will.

This be the verse you gave for me:
"Here he lies where he longed to be;
Home is the sailor, home from the sea,
And the hunter home from the hill."

ROBERT LOUIS STEVENSON

We are born for a higher destiny than that of earth; there is a realm where the rainbow never fades, where the stars will be spread before us like islands that slumber on the ocean, and where the beings that pass before us like shadows will stay in our presence forever.

EDWARD BULWER-LYTTON

WAITING

Serene, I fold my hands and wait,
Nor care for wind, or tide, or sea;
I rave no more 'gainst Time or Fate,
For, lo! my own shall come to me.

I stay my haste, I make delays,
For what avails this eager pace?
I stand amid the eternal ways,
And what is mine shall know my face.

Asleep, awake, by night or day,
The friends I seek are seeking me;
No wind can drive my bark astray,
Nor change the tide of destiny.

What matters if I stand alone?
I wait with joy the coming years;
My heart shall reap where it has sown,
And garner up its fruits of tears.

The waters know their own and draw
The brook that springs in yonder heights;
So flows the good with equal law
Unto the soul of pure delights.

The stars come nightly to the sky;
The tidal wave unto the sea;
Nor time, nor space, nor deep, nor high,
Can keep my own away from me.

JOHN BURROUGHS

EVENING PRAYER

Oh, God, Great Architect of the universe, protect us the day long
of this earthly life, that when the shadows lengthen, and the evening
comes; and the busy world is hushed; and the fever of our life is
ended; and our work on earth is done; then, of Thy tender mercy
grant us and all Masons where ever they may be, a safe lodging and
a holy rest and peace at the last forever.

PIERRE HARROWER

INDEX

270